THE BOOK OF
DONKEYS

Also by Donna Campbell Smith

The Book of Mules
The Book of Draft Horses
The Book of Miniature Horses

THE BOOK OF
DONKEYS

A GUIDE TO SELECTING, CARING, AND TRAINING

DONNA CAMPBELL SMITH

Guilford, Connecticut

An imprint of Rowman & Littlefield
Distributed by NATIONAL BOOK NETWORK

British Library Cataloguing in Publication Information Available

Library of Congress Cataloging-in-Publication Data is available

ISBN 978-1-4930-1768-3 (paperback)
ISBN 978-1-4930-2537-4 (e-book)

♾™ The paper used in this publication meets the minimum
requirements of American National Standard for Information
Sciences—Permanence of Paper for Printed Library Materials,
ANSI/NISO Z39.48-1992.

CONTENTS

ACKNOWLEDGMENTS

I always meet the nicest folks while I am writing about the animals they love. Donkey folks are right up there at the top when it comes to being friendly and helpful. Thanks to social media I have met donkey experts who have shared their knowledge, photographs, and enthusiasm with me, a complete stranger. I am grateful to each one of you who have taken time to chat with me about donkeys, sharing your expertise and photographs. In the real world I send special thanks to those who gave their time for me to come out and take pictures. It was a complete delight photographing your donkeys.

Shannon Hoffman gets her own paragraph. After all the help she gave me while writing *The Book of Mules*, she is the first person I turned to when I began writing *The Book of Donkeys*. Shannon has once again been so very gracious in letting me take up her time to answer questions and let me photograph her donkey at her farm, Red St. Clair. She invited me to her two-day Obstacle and Horsemanship Boot Camp where she introduced me to her friends with donkeys. They patiently allowed me to photograph their beautiful donkeys for which I am thankful. Shannon also introduced me to her farrier, Craig Horvath, who let me take pictures while he worked and answered my hoof questions.

Rita Rosenkranz, I am very fortunate to have you looking out for me; you are everything I could hope for in an agent. Thank you, Holly Rubino, for saying "Yes," and Lynn Zelem, for your expert editing.

Ladies of Second Cup Writers Group, what would I do without your encouragement and inspiration? We've been together for nine years. You are my sisters.

My wonderful, beautiful family: Dineane, bless you for plowing through and editing my first draft. Julia, Deborah, and Jessica, thank you for bearing with me and for being the best cheerleaders in the world. I am so blessed.

PREFACE

I am going to admit right up front that while I have owned more horses than I can remember in my lifetime, I have never owned a donkey. I have had to answer the fair question, "How can you write a book about donkeys if you've never had one?" more than once on social media while writing this book.

I didn't mind answering, because, like I said, it is a fair question if you're not a writer. On the other hand, writers write about a lot of things with which they do not have personal experience. I have good research skills, if I do say so myself, and I know a lot of folks who do have donkeys. I've interviewed owners and written articles about donkeys, and photographed and petted my share of donkeys. I have worked in the horse industry for about three decades and earned an AAS degree in equine technology. So, I do have plenty of equine experience. And, yes, I am well aware that a donkey is not a horse with long ears. But, there are enough similarities that I believe my decades of horse management count for something.

I've been searching my mental files to remember donkeys that crossed my path in all my sixty-eight years. I think the first place I learned about donkeys were those in the Bible stories my mother read to me when I was a small child. I knew Mary rode a donkey to Bethlehem, and one of the most fantastical donkeys in the Bible, or of all donkey history, was Balaam's talking donkey.

The next donkey I can remember was Eeyore in the *Winnie the Pooh* books. Later, I watched the books come alive in animated film. I could relate to Eeyore, being prone to a little gloominess at times myself. Now that I have met many real donkeys and their owners I am feeling that tug at my heart strings. If I were younger, I would have to have a donkey. They have a unique personality that definitely is unlike any horse I've ever owned. I have met donkeys who seemed to find me tolerable as I snapped picture after picture of them. Some have nibbled on my shirttail, and the hardest part about taking their pictures was getting far enough away to get more than an ear in the frame. Some were so curious about what I was doing that they practically got in my lap. They seem to genuinely enjoy human attention, so how can you not enjoy giving it to them?

Donkeys are hard workers, don't talk back to their bosses, and don't gossip behind their backs. There are millions of donkeys in the world helping humans survive. Here in the United States, more and more folks are finding donkeys are trustworthy partners on the trail or fun buddies to hang out with at home. I think we can all learn a few things from donkeys: patience, humor, steadfastness, and courage to name just a few.

> *I believe I would rather ride a donkey than any beast in the world. He goes briskly, he puts on no airs, he is docile, though opinionated. Satan himself could not scare him, and he is convenient—very convenient. When you are tired riding you can rest your feet on the ground and let him gallop from under you.*
>
> —*Mark Twain,* The Innocents Abroad

CHAPTER ONE

ORIGIN AND HISTORY

THE EARLIEST ANCESTORS OF THE HORSE AND ASS CAME ON the scene sixty-five million years ago. This small equid, *Eohippus*, roamed the forests of North America and spread from there all over the world to North and South America, Asia, Europe, and Africa. They all disappeared from the Americas by the end of the ice age about ten thousand years ago. It is theorized that the extinction of the horse from the Americas was due to either loss of their food source, due to climate change, or overhunting by human beings.

People first used asses and horses for food and the hides for shelters and clothing. Donkeys were first domesticated as long as five thousand years ago in Africa. Nubian and Somalian asses, subspecies of African wild asses (*Equus africanus*), were once thought to be the ancestor of today's domestic donkey. But modern DNA research has shown that the Somali wild ass is not one of the ancestors of the domestic donkey, while confirming today's donkey is related to the Nubian ass. Researchers believe humans domesticated the Nubian several times throughout ancient history.

The Somali ass is currently an endangered species with no more than a thousand left in the wild. It is a subspecies of the African wild ass that is native to the desert areas of Eritrea and Ethiopia. They are gray with lighter bellies, distinct zebra stripes on the lower legs, a dark mane, and dark tips on their ears.

The Asian wild ass or onager (*Equus hemionus*) is native to central Asia. The subspecies Syrian onager is extinct, and other species of onager are endangered. Onagers, also called half asses or stilt-legged asses, have longer legs than other asses. They do not have shoulder or leg stripes but some do have a dark dorsal stripe. The Asian wild ass has no known domestic relatives.

EARLY DOMESTICATION

Pictorial records and skeletal remains show Egyptians domesticated donkeys about 3400 BC. Some believe Nubian shepherds used donkeys as pack animals even earlier than that. Wealthy people of Egypt owned as many as a thousand donkeys. They were used in agriculture for their milk and meat like other livestock and as pack animals. This greatly enhanced the trade enterprises for Egypt with surrounding countries. Archeologists have found remains of donkeys in Egyptian royal tombs, indicating the value of their donkeys.

By 1000 BC donkeys were being used in southwestern Asia chiefly to breed mules, crossed with horses or Asian asses to produce larger and more powerful animals for transporting goods and riding.

Evidence of the domesticated donkey's move into the Middle East can be found in the Old and New Testaments of the Bible

Farmers with ass, Egyptian art inside a grave chamber.
Egyptians domesticated donkeys about 3400 BC.

in numerous passages, dating back as far as 1400 BC. In Genesis 12:16 Abram listed among his wealth female donkeys. Donkeys were counted as possessions of the wealthy in Genesis many times, and in the Ten Commandments the donkey is listed with the possessions of a neighbor that one should not covet. In Exodus we read that Moses put his wife and sons on a donkey to go back to Egypt. An account of King Saul searching for his father's lost donkeys can be found in I Samuel 9:3. There are many references to using donkeys for packing throughout the Old Testament.

We read in II Samuel 16:1, "When David had gone a short distance beyond the summit, there was Ziba, the steward of Mephibosheth, waiting to meet him. He had a string of donkeys saddled and loaded with two hundred loaves of bread, a hundred cakes of raisins, a hundred cakes of figs and a skin of wine." One of the best known donkey references in the New Testament is in the Gospels, where we read that Mary rode a donkey into Bethlehem just before the birth of Jesus. In John 12:14 we read of Jesus's ride on a donkey on Palm Sunday. All of this lets us know that the donkey was highly valued throughout Western Asia.

By 2000 BC donkeys had been introduced to Europe, where they were used for transportation and for producing mules. The donkeys were most likely brought to Europe by the Romans as they made their conquests into Spain, Hungary, Germany, and finally Great Britain. After the fall of the Roman Empire donkeys all but disappeared from most of Europe. The Mediterranean vineyard and olive orchard keepers continued to find the donkey useful in their farming operations. Their surefootedness made them especially good pack animals in mountainous terrain.

The donkey was eventually brought back to central Europe by monks who used them for farming and turning millstones to grind grain into flour.

DONKEYS IN AMERICA

Columbus is credited with introducing the donkey to the New World. In a letter he wrote to King Ferdinand and Queen Isabella in January 1494 during his second voyage, he asked for supplies. Included in the list of things needed were "some he-asses and she-asses and some mares for labor and breeding, as there are none of these animals here of any value or which can be made of use by man." In several writings it is recorded that during his second voyage (1493-1496) he brought four jacks and two jennies to Hispaniola to be used to breed mules, which are a hybrid cross between donkeys and horses. Explorers after Columbus brought donkeys to South and Central America. Soon a large number of donkeys populated those regions. Donkeys were valued for their stamina and ability to go long distances carrying heavy loads. The native people began to appreciate their value for transportation and packing.

It is believed that donkeys were first brought from Mexico to Arizona in 1598 by Juan de Onate, a Spanish conquistador, to use while he was exploring the Great Plains and lower Colorado River area. Donkeys continued to spread northward from Mexico, eventually reaching Canada.

Donkeys were used in Canada to transport freight from Alberta to British Columbia. They played a role during the Yukon Gold Rush as a beast of burden. Photographs from that era show donkeys being used to haul lumber and prospecting supplies.

By the time of the American Revolution donkeys were being used by the colonists to pull carts, aid in farm work, and breed mules. While George Washington is given credit for being the first to use donkeys for breeding mules, donkeys most assuredly had arrived on the scene long before Washington's interest in raising the donkey-horse hybrids. Large donkeys, predecessors of the American mammoth donkey, were developed from imported European asses in the eighteenth century.

In the west and north donkeys were used by loggers and fur trad-ers. It was during the gold-rush days of the late 1800s when donkeys reached their heyday in the American West. Donkeys were shipped to the United States to be used in various mining operations such as packing ore out of the mines and turning the ore-grinding mills. The picture of the lone gold prospector leading his pack burro has become an icon of the gold-rush days. Once mining became mech-anized the donkeys were of no use. Many were let loose to fend for themselves. Their descendants can still be found ranging free in the deserts of the Western United States today.

British consul Richard Chalton imported the first donkeys to Hawaii in 1824. They were used on plantations to haul coffee, taro, rice, papayas, and other crops. The Hawaiian donkeys were called "nightingales." Most people could only afford one donkey. Donkeys, being the social creatures they are, do not like being alone. So, when the day's work was over and the donkeys were taken home with their owners, they didn't like being separated from the other donkeys. They would call to neighboring donkeys all through the night. This concert of donkey braying apparently sounded like music to the island people, and they dubbed them the nightingale donkeys.

After World War II the Hawaiian donkeys were replaced with army-surplus Jeeps. No longer useful, the donkeys were abandoned. Being the survivors they are, the donkeys flourished on their own and multiplied. A large number of them have been relocated to preserves on the mainland over the years, while some of their descendants still exist in the wild in Hawaii.

Donkeys were still being used for mining in the twentieth cen-tury in isolated instances in the United States. An example were the donkeys of the Detroit Salt Mines. Constructed in 1910, Detroit Salt and Manufacturing Company lies one thousand feet deep beneath the city of Detroit. In the early days donkeys and mules were low-ered into the mines with ropes. The animals spent their entire lives working below the surface of the mine. Small donkeys were also still being used in pit-mining operations of the eastern United States to transport coal to the surface, pulling carts in and out of the mines.

In Great Britain donkeys were used in coal mines as recently as the 1980s. Donkeys are still being used in mining in other parts of the world.

Later in twentieth-century America, as mechanism replaced them, donkeys became a mere novelty, mainly sold as pets. Small burros could be ordered from the Sears and Roebuck, Spiegel, and Montgomery Ward catalogs as late as the 1950s. In the 1955 Spiegel catalog, "Lovable Mexican Burros" are described as an "extremely intelligent, soft eyed little fellow from South-of-the-Border. Gentle and extra tame, friendly to other animals." The burros being sold were three to eight months old, and the shipping weight was 125 pounds. The price was $69.95.

Large donkeys continued to be used for breeding mules, which were still used to some extent in farming and by the military. By mid-century, farming with mules finally gave way to tractors, causing both the donkey and mule populations to dwindle to their lowest point.

Donkeys are currently making a comeback, becoming more popular in twenty-first century America for recreational use, mainly trail riding and packing trips. Donkeys are still in demand for producing mules, as mules are also seeing an increase in demand. Both species are valued for their stamina, surefootedness, and intelligence.

CHAPTER TWO

DONKEYS IN ART, ENTERTAINMENT, AND POLITICS

THE WALLS OF COSQUER CAVE IN MARSEILLES, FRANCE, ARE adorned with prehistoric paintings, some of which picture wild donkeys. The cave, discovered in 1985, is below sea level and can only be accessed by divers. The paintings are believed to be 27,000 years old.

In ancient times the donkey was a symbol of peace and humility. Donkeys are pictured in the art of ancient Egypt, other parts of Africa, Asia, and the Mediterranean.

Biblical art often features the donkey in stories of Old and New Testaments. Rembrandt's painting, *Balaam and the Ass*, illustrates

Donkey illustration from thirteenth-century France/ Flanders, artist unknown.

Balaam and the Ass by Rembrandt.

the story told in Numbers about Balaam's talking donkey. Rembrandt's *Flight into Egypt* (1627) is another of his many works that include the donkey. The donkey is shown in paintings of the nativity, Mary riding a donkey to Bethlehem, and Jesus riding a donkey into Jerusalem on what is now commemorated as Palm Sunday.

Vincent Van Gogh used a donkey as the subject of several of his drawings. His painting, *Morning with Farmer and Pitchfork; His Wife Riding a Donkey and Carrying a Basket*, shows the farmer's wife riding a donkey. *The Donkey Ride* by impressionist Eva Gonzalès pictures a lady sitting side-saddle on a donkey with a man leaning on the donkey's neck talking to her. Jan Verhas, a Belgian artist of the 1800s, is well known for his paintings of children riding donkeys on the beach.

Private Simpson, D.C.M., & his donkey at Anzac was painted by Horace Moore-Jones. He was inspired by a photograph taken of a field medic using a donkey to transport a wounded soldier to safety in the World War I battle at Gallipoli. He painted at least two versions and the image became famous world-wide. It is also known as *Man with a Donkey*.

The donkey as a subject in modern art includes Picasso's portrait of his son, *Paulo on a Donkey*, and the beautiful *Woman on a Donkey*. Jackson Pollock's abstract *Composition with Donkey Head* and Salvador Dalí's *The Rotting Donkey* are examples of giants in modern art whose work included donkeys as a subject. Many more modern-day artists have painted and sculpted donkeys throughout the world.

THE DONKEY IN LITERATURE

It was in Mesopotamia and Egypt that humans invented the written language around 3200 BC, about the same time and place that donkeys were domesticated. So, it is logical that the donkey was written into the earliest literature. Donkeys show up in Egyptian mythology and folklore. The sun god Ra was symbolized as a donkey.

Donkeys are mentioned many times in the Old Testament, but one of the most memorable stories is the one about Balaam's donkey. The story can be found in Numbers 22:21–39. Balaam was on his way, riding his donkey, to meet with Moabite officials. God sent an armed angel to stop him. Balaam could not see the angel in his path, but the donkey did and shied away from it. Balaam beat his donkey. After the third instance of the angel stopping the donkey and the donkey getting a beating, God allowed the donkey to speak to Balaam. After a short exchange between the donkey and Balaam, God let Balaam see the angel. Only then did he concede he'd treated the donkey badly and Balaam listened to God's message.

Aesop features donkeys in at least twenty of his fables. In one he tells the tale of an ass that puts on a lion's skin to scare the other creatures. The fox finds him out when he hears the donkey braying. The moral of the story is, you can't judge one by their looks.

Islamic tradition gives us the story titled "The Conversation of the Donkey," which is found in the book *The Beginning and the End*, written by Ibn Kathir, in which Muhammad and the donkey, Ya'foor, talk to one another. The donkey plays a role in Christian literature, including the humble donkey that Mary rode to Bethlehem where the baby Jesus was to be born.

It is written that a donkey provided transportation for the adult William Shakespeare. He included a part for a donkey in one of his plays, *A Midsummer Night's Dream*. In the play, Bottom, first a human, is later transformed into an ass.

In the novel *The Swiss Family Robinson*, by Johann David Wyss, a donkey named Robert survives the shipwreck with the family. They use him as a pack animal. Robert meets a wild ass and they produce offspring, but later Robert meets his demise when he is swallowed by a boa constrictor.

In George Orwell's *Animal Farm*, we meet Benjamin, the fatalistic donkey who is uninterested in the pigs' rebellious plot because he believes life will still be unpleasant no matter who is in charge.

Swiss Family Robinson, 1883 illustration
of a boa killing the donkey.

His donkey personality is similar to that of Eeyore in A. A. Milne's *Winnie the Pooh* books, first published in 1924. Eeyore is smart, but also has a gloomy outlook on life, expecting the worst to happen in most situations. In spite of that personality trait he is portrayed as a kind and faithful friend.

Marguerite Henry's *Brighty of the Grand Canyon* depicts the little burro as brave and loyal. The book was based on a true story told in 1890. The real "Brighty" was found abandoned and later was used at the Grand Canyon to carry water for tourists. He became very popular, especially with the children, because of his sweet disposition. A movie was made in 1967 based on the book, and in 1982 the image of the donkey was released as a Breyer model.

These are just a few classic books in which donkeys are either main or supporting characters. A quick browse in the library or bookstore will reveal many more.

DONKEYS IN FILM

Donkeys in the movies are mostly of the animated genre. Disney's donkeys include Alexander in *Pinocchio*, Jacchus in 1940's *Fantasia*, Burrito the flying donkey in 1944's *The Three Caballeros*, the Three Donkeys in *The Small One*, and Jenny the Burro, appearing in 1942 in *The Village Smithy* and *Donald's Gold Mine*. The literary favorites Eeyore and Brighty also appeared in film versions of their stories. A more recent invention is the popular donkey named Donkey in the *Shrek* movies.

The hit 1970s TV show *Grizzly Adams* had a donkey star named Number 7. Number 7 was sidekick to mountain man Mad Jack, played by Denver Pyle. The part of Number 7 was actually played by several burros; one in particular was used for braying.

DONKEYS IN POLITICS

As the symbol of the Democratic Party, donkeys appear on posters and political ads during election years. It all started with Andrew Jackson's race against John Quincy Adams in 1828. Adams called Jackson a jackass, meaning it as an insult. Jackson found the label humorous and turned the tables by putting the donkey in a favorable light—pointing out the donkey-like qualities of loyalty, determination, and the ability to carry heavy loads. He put images of the donkey on his campaign posters.

Thomas Nast is given credit for making the donkey image stick as the symbol of the Democratic Party with a political cartoon titled, "A Live Jackass Kicking a Dead Lion." The cartoon appeared in *Harper's Weekly* magazine in 1870. He continued using the donkey as the Democratic symbol in other cartoons. By 1880 other cartoonists were drawing the donkey into their work and the donkey became known as the Democratic mascot all over the country. It remains so today.

ENTERTAINMENT AND SPORTS

According to an article in a 1954 issue of *Popular Mechanics*, the game of donkey ball originated in early mining camps. The miners had Sundays off and they played baseball mounted on the donkeys that they used to haul ore out of the mines during the week. Riding donkey-back added a fun twist to the game.

Today donkey ball usually means donkey basketball. Donkey basketball began in the Midwest in the 1930s. It was cheap entertainment during the Great Depression. Traveling donkey-ball troupes went from town to town playing the game before enthusiastic audiences.

The game is played loosely like regular basketball, but with two teams of four. The teams are made up of townspeople where the event is being held. The riders are required to wear safety helmets. The donkeys are ridden with halters and rope reins and are fitted with rubber shoes to protect the gymnasium floors where the games are played. Rules forbid striking the donkeys or pulling on their ears, tail, or hair.

PETA and many other animal-rights groups are very much against donkey ball, identifying it as inhumane. In spite of the controversy, many schools and groups across the country use donkey-ball games as fund-raisers.

Donkeys have been popular performers in circuses and traveling entertainment troupes for centuries. Four donkeys traveled with Buffalo Bill's Wild West Show across the Atlantic when they sailed for the show's European tour.

Clowns with donkeys have been a popular circus act for a long time. One of those acts was Lew F. Sunlin and his two donkeys,

Peanut and Pickle. While he was touring with the Irin Bros. circus in 1891, a fire destroyed the circus train's stock car, killing Peanut. Pickles was saved. The *New York Dramatic News* reported later the same month that Sunlin bought another donkey and would have it ready to perform in ten days. The popular act toured with the Ringling Bros. for several seasons.

Whimsical Walker was a popular clown in the mid-1800s. He was famous for his animal acts, and trained two donkeys in his career. One, a donkey called Tom, he taught to sit in a chair and sing *Home Sweet Home*.

Today donkeys are still performing with such prestigious circuses as Ringling Bros., usually teamed up with the clowns in humorous acts, or working at liberty in the ring.

Donkeys, especially miniature donkeys, make entertaining pets for children. They are generally docile and just plain cute. Many times they are trained to pull a cart and do tricks. They are popular in petting zoos and for giving children rides at festivals and fairs. Donkey rides have been a popular children's activity on beaches of the United Kingdom since the late 1800s. In recent years laws have been put into place to protect the donkeys from being overworked, such as limits on the weight they can carry and hours of use. The donkeys must have breaks and also have one full day off from giving rides.

Most donkey owners will agree that the donkey is perhaps second only to the dog as a faithful and entertaining companion to their human partners.

CHAPTER THREE

BREEDS AND TYPES

DONKEYS IN AMERICA ARE CLASSED BY SIZE (MINIATURE, STAN-dard, and mammoth) rather than by breeds. Donkeys were initially brought to America by explorers to use in transporting goods and people. Donkeys first arrived in America in Hispaniola in 1495 on a supply ship ordered by Columbus. During the colonial period larger donkeys were in demand for breeding with horses to produce mules for farming and transporting goods. George Washington is given credit by some historians as being the first to breed donkeys and mules in America, but it is more likely he just got more attention than some others. In 1785 he was gifted two jacks by Spain's King Charles III, but only one survived the voyage. Washington received two more, one from the Mediterranean island of Malta and another from South America, and some female donkeys as well. They were used predominantly for raising mules. But these were not the only donkeys imported to America in the 1700s.

There are American associations striving to keep records and pedigrees for certain breeds, including the National Miniature Donkey Association, American Council of Spotted Asses, American Donkey and Mule Society, the Canadian Donkey and Mule Association, and American Mammoth Jackstock Registry.

DONKEY CHARACTERISTICS

According to a donkey fact sheet published by the Department of Agriculture and Rural Development of Alberta, Canada, donkeys'

Donkey characteristics include long ears, a large head, and a short mane.

"larger brain capacity is evidenced by the fact that donkeys require bridles with a larger browband than that needed for a comparable size of horse or pony. Donkeys are reported to have developed an intelligence superior to that of horses, but its instincts give rise of different behavior, in certain circumstances, which many misconstrue as stubbornness. For example, it is not the nature of the donkey to run in panic when frightened as the horse instinctively does. Under the same conditions donkeys are more likely to stop, stand still and study the situation carefully to determine the best course of action."

The American Donkey and Mule Society also describes the donkey as laid back and self-preserving in nature, not always doing what the human thinks is best. The donkey is characterized as very friendly and excellent around children.

The most noticeable and unique physical characteristic of the donkey is its ears. They are much longer than those of a horse. The donkey's desert origins made this characteristic necessary; they keep the animal cool as blood circulates through the vessel in the ears. The long ears also help donkeys hear over long distances. Some donkeys' ears flop to the side, while others are upright.

The donkey's head is large with a wide brow and large eyes, giving it a wide field of vision. A straight, roman, or dished profile is acceptable. The upper and lower teeth should meet evenly. The neck tends to be straight, the withers low, and the back short and straight. The hindquarters are not as round as those of a horse. The donkey stands higher at the hip; the bones are longer and more angular than a horse, with longer and smoother muscles.

The hair on most donkeys is coarse, with the exception of some breeds such as the Poitou that has long, silky hair. The mane is also coarse and usually stands up. The donkey does not have a forelock. The tail is covered in short hair until reaching the end in a tuft of longer hairs, much like a cow's tail.

The donkey's hooves are round, tough, and elastic. They seldom need shoes unless the donkey is being worked or ridden on particularly rocky ground. The pasterns are upright to match the more upright angle of the hooves. Ideally the shoulder is sloped, well-muscled, and strong. The legs are straight and in proportion to the body type of the donkey. The hindquarters are also strong and well-muscled. The donkey's movement should be true of gait, free, and with a good ground-covering stride.

The jennet's conformation should present a feminine character, being more refined about the head and neck and longer bodied than the jack. (The female donkey is called a jennet or a jenny, while the intact male is a jack, and a castrated male is a gelding.)

AMERICAN SPOTTED ASSES

Spotted donkeys come in all sizes. Most are miniature, small standard, or standard sized, usually with a background color of gray

Spotted donkey, Molly, owned by Bob Radcliff.

or dun. A few mammoth donkeys are spotted, usually with a black background.

When breeding with the hope of spotted offspring, one should keep in mind that two solid parents never have spotted offspring. At least one parent must have spots; the grandparents do not factor in. A blaze face counts as being spotted. Breeding a spotted donkey to a non-spotted will result in a spotted foal about 50 percent of the time. Breeding a spotted to a spotted donkey raises the odds to about two-thirds of the time.

In 1967 Dave Parker and John Conter created the American Council of Spotted Asses and a registry for spotted donkeys. The only requirement for registration is that the donkey have at least two spots occurring behind the throatlatch and above the legs that are visible in a photograph.

MAMMOTH DONKEYS

The American mammoth was developed by selective breeding from five main breeds: Andalusian, Majorcan, Catalonian, Maltese, and Poitou. Standard donkeys were also used in developing the mammoth. The mammoth was, and still is, used predominately for mule production. The fine bone structure of the Majorcan made ideal crosses for riding mules. The Andalusian with its heavier bone made a good cross for a draft type animal. Each of the breeds offered a characteristic that over time resulted in the impressive large donkey of today.

When the American Mammoth Jackstock Registry was first set up, black was the only acceptable color. That has changed over time and other colors, sorrel in particular, are accepted. The desirable characteristics of the American mammoth are a well-shaped head that tapers to a round muzzle and a nicely muscled neck that is not too thick. The body should have good width, depth, and length,

Mammoth donkey.

strong loins, and a full hip. The legs are thick and strong, and the feet large and well cupped. The jacks must measure at least fifty-six inches at the withers, and the jennets should measure at least fifty-four inches.

MINIATURE DONKEYS

The smallest of the donkey family is the miniature Mediterranean donkey. Their small size and gentle disposition make them ideal pets and show animals. These little donkeys first appeared in history in Northern Africa. It is not known how or by whom, but the miniature donkeys later made their way to the island of Sardinia, and from there to Sicily, both islands off the western coast of Italy. Tourists from around the world, especially North America and Europe, were

Miniature jennet.

smitten by these diminutive and sweet-tempered donkeys. Now there are only a few miniature donkeys left in the Mediterranean. The highest number is found in North America.

Robert Green, a stockbroker from New York, is credited with first importing the miniature donkey to American from Sardinia in 1929. He started with seven donkeys on his farm in New Jersey, but three were killed by dogs. Three jennets, Miranda, Palermo, and Suzanne, and one jack, Impheus, survived the attack. Mr. Green's first foal was born on Columbus Day 1929; he named it Christopher Columbus. Green had a large collection of carts and other vehicles he used for driving the miniature donkeys. By 1935 he had fifty-two donkeys in his herd. He kept most of them, only selling a few to stabilize the size of his herd.

The Miniature Donkey Registry was founded in 1958 by Bea Langfeld. She'd purchased a miniature donkey as a pet for her daughter who had cerebral palsy. The Langfelds went on to raise show-quality miniature donkeys on their ranch in Omaha, Nebraska. Mrs. Langfeld turned the administration of the registry over to the American Donkey and Mule Society in 1987 when the job became too much for her to handle alone. Mrs. Langfeld had by then compiled the most complete records of the miniature Mediterranean donkey in the world.

The National Miniature Donkey Association (NMDA) was founded in 1989. The organization sanctions shows, keeps a list of sanctioned judges, developed a rule book, and keeps records of show results. They have also produced educational materials and implemented a DNA testing/typing program and a gelding incentive program. They have set the standard for the miniature donkey as a breed.

The maximum height according to the standards set by the association is thirty-six inches at maturity, which is three years old. The general appearance of a miniature donkey as set by NMDA is as follows: "The Miniature Donkey should be attractive, sound, strong and sturdy. The animal should be well balanced as the various parts blend together in a nicely coupled, compact picture. The animal should have an alert expression and 'presence'; jennets should look feminine and slightly more refined and jacks should be relatively stocky and masculine."

The International Miniature Donkey Registry was formed in 1992. They have two height classifications: Class A for donkeys 36 inches and under and Class B for donkeys 36.1 inches up to 38 inches.

Several hundred miniature Mediterranean donkeys have been imported to the United Kingdom from the United States and Canada. The Miniature Mediterranean Donkey Association (MMDA) maintains the miniature donkey studbook of the UK. The MMDA studbook will only accept donkeys with at least three recorded and numbered generations in their pedigrees. The MMDA general registry will accept donkeys with at least one registered and numbered generation in their pedigrees.

STANDARD DONKEYS

The mid-sized donkey is classified as the standard donkey and is the most common donkey worldwide. They are used for riding, packing, working, and showing.

Standard donkeys are further divided into small standards (36.01 to 40 inches), standard donkeys (40.01 to 48 inches), and large standards (48.01 to 54 inches for jennets or 56 inches for jacks). Standard donkeys may be registered with the American Donkey and Mule Society.

Standard donkey.

DONKEYS AROUND THE WORLD

African Donkeys

Donkeys are very important possessions in most African nations, but breed purity is not a high priority for most in Africa. Donkeys are used for working and families depend on them for their livelihood. In her article "Donkeys in Africa," Linda Purdy wrote, "It is interesting to note that the donkeys owned by a rural family are most often cared for by the women. If not for the donkey, the women become the beasts of burden, whereupon they weaken under the work load and often sicken and die, devastating or completely destroying the family unit. In Ethiopia, when a donkey dies, the women cling together and weep."

African ass.

Still, the donkey in Africa is often overworked and neglected. Many die of malnutrition and parasite infestation. Several organizations are working to teach farmers better donkey husbandry.

The African wild ass is the foundation for all domestic breeds of donkey. Their color ranges from gray to chestnut with white legs and underbelly. They have a dark dorsal stripe, and some have zebra-like striped legs. They are critically endangered, with fewer than six hundred left. They have been overhunted for meat and have suffered from loss of habitat as they compete with domestic livestock for grazing and water.

The Abyssinian donkey, also known as the Ethiopian donkey, is a small donkey standing only nine hands or under. Most are gray, while some are chestnut. They are used as work animals in Ethiopia.

Australian Donkeys

Founded in 1976, the English Donkey Society of Australia seeks to keep as pure as possible the English and Irish type donkey and to maintain breeding records. The maximum height of these donkeys is eleven hands.

The Australian teamster donkey, named for its original purpose as a wagon donkey and for its place in early Australian history, has been developed over the past 150 years. The registry was formally created in 2005. Most are large standard in size. Some early records suggest they are of Andalusian ancestry. There is also evidence of American jackstock heritage.

European Donkeys

France

The Poitou was developed in the Poitou region of western France more than a thousand years ago. It was 1184 when the Poitou studbook was established. The main purpose of the Poitou has been the production of mules to be used both for work and riding. The Poitou

Poitou donkey. *Photo by Père Igor*

was almost wiped out after World War II when mechanization made mules obsolete. By 1980 there were only eighty purebred Poitou donkeys left in the world. Efforts to preserve the breed began in the late 1900s. In 2012 about 2,500 purebred Poitou were added to the studbook.

Poitou were imported to America in the 1800s and 1900s and crossed with other donkeys to produce the mammoth jack. Today there are many donkeys in America with Poitou characteristics, but they cannot be registered if there are no papers proving their lineage. The American Livestock Conservancy lists the status of the Poitou as "critical." The Hamilton Rare Breeds Foundation in Hartland, Vermont, was founded by Debbie Hamilton in 1996. They are using frozen semen imported from French herds to produce Baudet du Poitou purebred offspring. Baudet means "sire of mules" which was originally the primary purpose of the breed. L'Association des Éleveurs des Races Équine, Mulassière et Asine, Baudet du Poitou is the registry organization responsible for registering purebred Poitou donkeys.

The Poitou stands fourteen to fifteen hands and weighs between 750 and 950 pounds. They have a large head and long ears and are well muscled and heavy boned, making them ideal to breed with horses for working mules. One of their most unique characteristics is their hair, which hangs in long dreadlocks. The only acceptable colors are black and dark brown. They can have no other color nor dorsal stripes.

The Cotentin donkey is found in Normandy, France. They are small, about eleven hands, gray with a shoulder stripe, and some have leg stripes. Colors not allowed are brown, bay, black, and white. Cotentins used to be found on every farm being used as pack animals, primarily to haul milk to market. Their numbers steadily declined in the twentieth century with the use of vehicles. In 1997 they were declared an official breed and the Association de l'âne du Cotentin (Association of the Cotentin Ass) began keeping records. The studbooks were closed, no longer accepting donkeys with unregistered parents, in 2001. There are currently about 1,200 registered Cotentin donkeys.

Italy

Italy has several donkey breeds. The miniature Mediterranean donkeys in America have their roots in Sicily and Sardinia. The Sardinian donkey is native to the island of Sardinia and is a very old breed. They were used like farm trucks, pulling carts to carry tools to and from the fields. They are only about thirty-three inches tall and are gray with a white underbelly and a dark cross over its shoulders. Numbers have dwindled from 27,000 in 1965 to a couple of hundred today.

The Pantelleria from the island of Pantelleria is near extinction. They were used in circuses and as work donkeys as well as for breeding mules. They are known for their speed and stamina, and they are gaited, making them very smooth to ride. They stand about fourteen hands, black or dark bay in color, and have a short, fine coat. In the 1990s efforts began to bring back the old breed standard and preserve the Pantelleria.

A donkey from the Amiata Mountains of Tuscany, the Amiata, is another endangered breed in Italy. They are slender and gray, with leg stripes and the shoulder cross. They are about 13.2 hands. In 2006 there were seven hundred registered with Anagraphic Register of the Amiata, which was formed in 1993. In 1997 the books were closed to jacks, while still accepting jennets.

The Martina Franca is native to Apulia in southern Italy. It is a hardy donkey acclimated to the extreme temperatures of the region. The largest breed of eight indigenous donkey breeds recognized by the Italian Ministry of Agriculture and Forestry, it is popular for breeding mules. It is also used for packing and other work. The Association of Breeders of the Murge Horse and the Donkey of Martina Franca, which was formed in 1990, oversees the registration of the breed. They are dark brown or black with light gray around the eyes, on the muzzle, and the underbelly. They stand 14.1 to 14.3 hands.

Spain

The Andaluz donkeys of Cordovan Spain were used by the military, and consequently records of their bloodlines were carefully preserved. The Andaluz is a large donkey, light gray in color, with fine hair. They are believed to be the oldest breed still in existence today. They are endangered, with only a few more than one hundred left.

The Catalan donkey is found in Catalonia, Spain, and traces back to Somalia. There are about four hundred registered today. They are black or bay with white around the eyes, muzzle, and underbelly. They are a bit smaller than the Andaluz.

Another large Spanish donkey is the Zamorano-Leonés found in Zamora and Leon. It is bay with white accents around the eye, muzzle, and belly. There are about one thousand registered.

Found in the north of Spain is the Asno de las Encartaciones. This donkey is small, about forty-seven inches, and bay in color. With fewer than one hundred left, they are in danger of becoming extinct.

Middle Eastern and Asian Donkeys

The Asiatic wild ass is native to the semi-desert regions in most of the central and southern plains of Iran and has spread to other countries. It is tan and gets darker in the summer, with white markings on the back of the rump and the underbelly. It has a stripe down the back that is bordered by white. They are about 12.2 hands tall. They are described as more horse-like in appearance than other donkeys and are very fast runners. There are five subspecies: the Mongolian wild ass, the Indian wild ass or khur, the Turkmenian kulan, the Syrian wild ass (which is already extinct), and the onager. They are classified as endangered with their numbers dwindling because of loss of habitat, poaching for meat and skins, and competition with domestic animals for grazing and water.

There are eighteen or more donkey breeds in China including the following: Taihang, Subei, Shanbei, Linxian, Kulun, Jinnan, Jiami, Huaibei, Biyang, Guanzhong, Guangling, Qinqyang, Qinghai,Yunnan, Yangyuan, and Xinjiang. Donkey farming is becoming more profitable than raising beef because imported beef has brought down prices for domestic beef. Donkey meat is popular in China, as are cosmetic and health products that are made from the skin, milk, and placenta. Chinese farmers are turning away from raising cattle and sheep in favor of donkeys.

South American Donkeys

The Paso Fino donkeys, called *burro Criollo Colombiano,* in Colombia, South America, have the same smooth, rapid four-beat gait as Paso Fino horses and are shown in Paso Fino horse shows. They are in high demand to breed with gaited mares to produce gaited mules.

Their origins are the Andalusian and Catalonian donkeys that Columbus brought to the New World on his second trip to America. After three hundred years they were abandoned. They have developed their own features due to climate, food, and environment resulting in a smaller and smooth-gaited donkey.

Luzma Osorio of Villa Luz in Colombia said, "In our ranch we have been trying for the last twenty years to preserve and improve the Colombian donkey." They have been very successful. Their champion jack, Cosaco De Villa Luz, produced the most champion mules in Colombia and passes his genetic qualities, including his gait, to both his donkey and mule offspring. He was declared the Best Donkey Stallion of All Time in 1997. After the death of Cosaco De Villa Luz, one of his sons, Carolo, now holds the title.

The Pega donkeys were developed southeast of Brazil, and then they spread throughout the Brazilian and Paraguayan territories. They are also gaited and sought after for breeding gaited mules. They have a more refined profile than American donkeys with long legs and a fine body. The Pega donkeys are white, gray, or cream colored and stand about twelve hands. The Brazilian Association of Pêga Donkey Breeders was founded August 15, 1947.

Controversy surrounds the donkeys on the Caribbean island of Bonaire. DNA testing conducted by Dr. Gus Cothran in 2014 showed that the donkeys are a perfect match to the presumed extinct Nubian donkey. The island donkeys are descended from those brought to the New World by explorers in the 1500s. According to the island government, the donkeys have become overpopulated and wander about towns, presenting a hazard to traffic. In November 2013 the government entered a donkey removal contract with the Donkey Sanctuary of Bonaire. Under the agreement, male donkeys are gelded and released. The pregnant jennets are kept at the sanctuary. The future of these donkeys is unsure.

Free-ranging donkeys on Grand Turk Island are popular with tourists, but also create problems. The donkeys were brought to the

Grand Turk Island free-roaming donkeys. *Photo courtesy of Tammy Winkel*

island in the early 1700s to be used by salt miners, better known as salt rakers. The salt rakers used the donkeys to haul salt they gathered from the natural salt ponds on the island to ships for export. When the donkeys were no longer needed for this work they were allowed to run free. Plans are being made to move the donkeys to a neighboring island in the Dominican Republic to be used on dairy farms. They will haul milk from remote farms to central milk tanks.

Donkeys around the world have been bred to adapt to a wide range of purposes. With so many types, sizes, and breeds to choose from there is surely a donkey to fit any particular need, whether it be for work or pleasure.

CHAPTER FOUR

OWNERSHIP: HOUSING, TRANSPORTATION, AND EQUIPMENT

BEFORE YOU BRING YOUR DONKEY HOME THERE IS A GREAT deal of preparation to be done. The most obvious step, but one that is often overlooked, is to be sure the place you plan to keep the donkey is zoned for keeping livestock. Find out if there are any environmental restrictions, easements, deed restrictions, or covenants on the state, county, or local levels. If you need to build a shelter, you will probably have to get a building permit.

The ideal donkey pasture has room to exercise but is not too lush.

Donkeys love a good spot to roll.

The size of the barn, outbuildings, and the turnout space all depend on the size and number of donkeys being kept. The donkey's purpose as well as the geographic location will also have some bearing on what kind of facility will be needed. A working or trail-riding donkey will do fine with a run-in shed for its shelter in temperate climates, while a barn with a stall and a wash pit will be more convenient for a show donkey.

The layout out of the facility, including placement of buildings, paddocks, and pastures will depend on access, drainage, convenience to water, and electricity. Also, consider room for expansion.

Donkeys need space to exercise for their physical and mental well-being. They also enjoy rolling, preferably in a sandy bare spot. In addition to being a good back scrub, rolling is a natural way to repel insects.

SHELTER

Donkeys can normally tolerate cold, but not cold and wet. For that reason they need shelter from rain and snow. Unlike horses, rain

A run-in shed is adequate shelter for a donkey.

does not roll off donkeys' backs. Their coats absorb melted snow and rain, soaking them down to their skin. When given their choice to be inside or out, most donkeys will opt to stay outside their shelters. In extreme winter conditions, as in ice and sub-freezing temperatures, especially with very young or old donkeys, closing them in a shelter is sensible. Donkeys are very stoic animals and often do not show signs of distress. In summer the shelter provides shade and relief from flies.

A three-sided shed will be adequate if positioned in the right location. It must have good ventilation and drainage, be convenient to access, and face away from prevailing winds.

A closed barn is more for human convenience than the welfare of the donkey. Still, there are times when being able to put the donkey in a closed stall can be necessary: medical care, feeding, or preparing for a show. Otherwise the donkey is much better off being able to come and go from shelter to paddock or pasture. A run-in shed can have a gate for confinement when needed in an emergency.

Bedding will be necessary if the donkeys stay in for a longer time than it takes to feed them. It helps absorb urine and prevents sores on hocks, fetlocks, or hips from the friction of rubbing on a hard surface when they lie down. Avoid shavings from hardwood trees, especially those from black walnut trees, because some species can cause laminitis. Clean straw is a popular bedding choice, although some donkeys will eat it. Bedding should be six to eight inches deep. When cleaning the stalls, pick out the manure, then rake dry bedding to the side and clean out the wet spot. Spread the bedding back out, adding more as needed.

Unique to housing for donkeys is having enough ear clearance. Some donkeys are sensitive about anything touching their ears. If the ceiling is too low, they will stand with their heads dropped to avoid having their ears touch the top of the stall.

The size of the shed depends on the size and number of donkeys. The front height should be at least ten feet and the back eight feet for the standard-size donkey. Large mammoth types will need more space, and the miniature can do fine with less.

The recommended depth of a run-in shed is twenty-four feet in order to provide protection from rain and snow. In any type of shelter, cross-ventilation is the most important design element. For a run-in shed, leave space between the top of the back wall and the roof. The air movement helps prevent respiratory disease and reduces fly population. Drop-down panels on the back and sides will provide even more ventilation in summer, and then can be closed in winter. A partially closed front can add protection from cold winter winds.

A Quonset-style hut is a low-cost and easy-to-construct shelter that is ideal for miniature donkeys or small standards. The hut is made of two four-foot-high, sixteen-foot-long cattle panels, six T-posts, and a twelve-by-sixteen tarp. Drive the T-posts into the ground, three on each side, 4 feet apart, with 10.5 feet between the two rows. Fasten the two panels together with wire, and then place the ends inside the posts and anchor them with wire at the bottom and sides. The panel forms an arch between the rows of T-posts. Stretch a tarp over the arch and secure it with cord to the panel frame. A second tarp across the back breaks the wind in winter, but can be removed in summer to allow ventilation.

OUTBUILDINGS

Hay and equipment should ideally be stored in separate structures from the donkey shelter. Because of dust and fire hazard, store hay away from the barn. The hay barn should protect the hay from the

Store tack in a secure room.

elements. Wet hay can become combustible and is a breeding place for mold. Mowers and tractors should also be stored out of donkey reach to prevent injury. Store tack, feed, and supplies either in a locked room in the barn or in a separate building if the donkey shelter is a run-in shed.

FENCES AND GATES

Good fences are the key to keeping the donkey home and out of trouble. Budget, labor, aesthetics, and above all safety determine the type of fence to use. The number of donkeys, amount of available space, and placement of the buildings help determine how much fencing is needed. The size of the donkey will be a deciding factor in the height of the fences and amount of exercise room it will need. There are a variety of materials and designs to choose from.

Many farm owners will use a more attractive and expensive fence in the front of the property and a less expensive fencing material at the back where passersby cannot see it. Wood, steel pipe, PVC, and woven wire are some of the materials most commonly used for fences. Barbed wire and high-tensile wire should not be used, since the donkey can become entangled in it and sustain severe injuries.

The gate to the paddock or pasture must be secure, safe, and easy to operate—for the human, but not the donkey. The gate must be wide enough to drive a truck and tractor through and for you to walk through while leading the donkey. In addition, it must be strong enough to withstand the donkey leaning on the gate, running into it, kicking it, or grazing underneath it. A heavy, long gate will be more difficult to handle and will need extra support to prevent warping and sagging. One solution to that problem is to mount a wheel on the bottom corner to keep the gate from dropping to the ground. This will make opening and closing it easier. Another way to support long gates is by attaching a cable from the upper corner of the opening end to the top of a higher post at the hinged end. A

Wooden board fences are attractive and secure.

Sturdy gates are a must.

turnbuckle placed at the center of the cable will allow you to take up any slack in the cable due to stretching.

TRANSPORTATION

When asked if there are different approaches to hauling a donkey rather that a horse, donkey and mule owner Shannon Hoffman said, "It is pretty much the same." It is important to train the donkey to load and ride in a trailer ahead of time. Introduce them to the trailer before they need to be hauled.

There are different opinions on whether to haul a donkey tied or not tied. Many owners advocate not tying, so the donkey can stand as it feels safest. Miniatures and small standards are better left untied as they are too short to tie comfortably. If hauling loose, be sure that all doors and gates are secured to prevent the donkey from getting out of the trailer.

If hauling more than one donkey, start with the most experienced and best-loading one first, as donkeys learn by observation. If

Trailer-loading: in he goes.

Getting a reward for a job well done.

they see a donkey behaving badly they may see the trailer as a dangerous place to enter and refuse to do so. Practice loading until the donkey goes in easily, and then take some short trips to acclimate the animal to the motion so that it learns to keep its balance.

When taking long trips, plan the route when traffic is at a minimum. Also avoid traveling in the heat of the day. Accelerate, brake, and turn slowly to avoid throwing the donkey off balance. Be sure to have a cell phone, fully charged, and the phone number of someone at each end of the trip who can help in an emergency. Limit travel time to no more than eight hours per day. Plan stopping places where there is space to unload the donkey safely, and that have water sources.

Trailer maintenance is the key to hauling donkeys safely. Before every trip the following inspections should be made:

- Tires and spare tire: check air, tread, and damage
- Floor boards: check for rot, replace as needed
- Lights: inside and outside trailer
- Brakes
- Welds, hinges, hitch
- Protruding screws, bolts or anything that can injure the donkey

At least annually check the following and make needed repairs:

- Framing and construction of trailer for rust and other damage
- Wiring and lights
- Lubrication
- Ramp and doors
- Wheels and tires

In addition, make sure the towing vehicle passes all safety checks and that it can meet the trailer manufacturer's towing capacity requirements. Have a spare tire for both vehicle and trailer, and carry along a spare halter and long lead rope, first aid kit, and a flashlight.

Rubber floor mats help prevent the donkey from slipping and absorb sound. Bedding can also be added to make cleaning the trailer easier. Remove the bedding and mats after hauling and clean the floor thoroughly to prevent rotting.

Certain state and federal regulations require a commercial license if the towing vehicle, trailer, and load exceed ten thousand pounds. It is important to check towing weight. This can be done at a grain elevator or a weigh station at large ag centers or feed stores. There are restrictions in various states to do with height, weight, and length of the towing rig. Always heed the sign at weigh stations, because authorities at these locations also check health papers, Coggins tests, registration papers, and drivers' licenses. Not stopping at weigh stations, or not having the proper paperwork, can result in stiff penalties.

Tack, Harness and Equipment

The most primary items of equipment needed are a halter and lead rope. A regular horse halter will not always do. A donkey's head is shaped much differently than a horse's. It is very large, with prominent brow ridges, and shorter than the horse's head, tapering down to a small muzzle. A horse halter that is big enough to fit the broad head will be too long, causing the noseband to hang off the end of the nose. One short enough will be too tight. Fortunately, donkey halters can be found online but are rarely stocked in the local tack shop or farm supply. Halters for miniature and small donkeys seem to be more available than those for larger donkeys.

Deb Collins Kidwell, owner of Lake Nowhere Mule and Donkey Farm, uses draft horse halters for her big donkeys. "We have had pretty good luck with rope halters for the American mammoth jacks, but still use nylon for the little babies. I replace the poll strap buckle with snaps, which makes a major difference," she explained. "They will stand still for you to put them on, but after they are on for a few minutes and you want to take them off, they may be fidgeting and it is tough to get the buckles undone without a battle. I use the nylon halters on the babies because the weight of the halter itself gets them used to having something on their face and the brass rings jingle, letting them get used to an unusual noise."

Donkeys have much less pronounced withers than do horses. For that reason saddle fitting can be difficult, but for most donkeys a horse saddle will work. Deb Collins Kidwell likes the Boz saddle because of its Spring Flex Air Flow tree. It is also light weight at twenty-five pounds. Other donkey owners like the Wintec synthetic saddles. It is a matter of preference and individual choice as donkeys come in many shapes and sizes. The important thing is that the saddle fit well. Many riders also use a crupper or breeching to keep the saddle from putting pressure on the donkey's withers and neck when going downhill and to keep the saddle from sliding forward. A

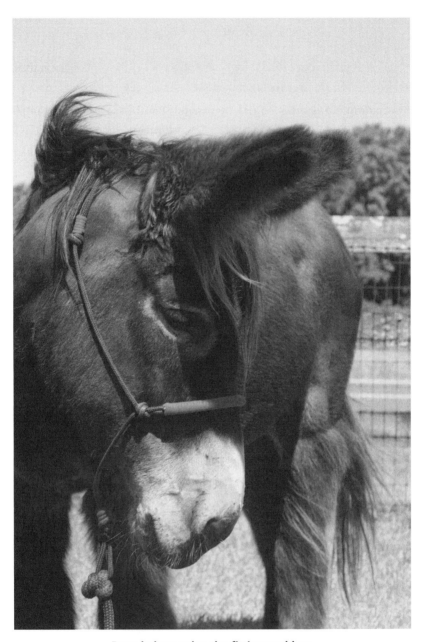

Rope halters solve the fitting problem.

**Breeching keeps the saddle from putting pressure on
the withers and neck when going downhill.**

back girth is used to keep the saddle from tilting up when riding in hilly terrain. It is important that all the rigging fit snugly to prevent saddle sores. The buckles and straps should be checked and adjusted every time they are used because the donkey's weight changes and the strapping stretches.

Because donkeys have bigger heads than horses it is important to measure the donkey and take the measurements with you to the tack store when shopping for a bridle.

Measure from the corner of the donkey's mouth on one side, up over the top of its head just behind the ears, and down the opposite side to the corner of the mouth.

Measure the throatlatch starting at the top of the head behind the ears, around the throat, and back up the other side to the top.

Measure for the browband from just behind the ears on one side, across the brow to the other ear.

If the bridle will have a noseband, measure the donkey around the nose about a thumb's width above the corners of the mouth.

Many donkeys are sensitive about their long ears. One bridle made with donkeys in mind is the Be Kind to Ears bridle. It has a snap-on crown piece that allows the entire crown piece to be opened to place behind the ears and then snapped closed, so that the ears don't have to be touched or bent.

Hoffman recommends that for older or ill-trained donkeys, owners use the bit that gives the best control in order to stay safe. The goal should always be to get them trained and working off the bit, then move down to a snaffle. That will not happen with every donkey. Some of them, once they learn they can grab the bit and get control, will always need a stronger bit.

"Of course, starting a young animal, or trying to start over, any type of snaffle bit is always good because it teaches them to give to direct pressure and if used correctly to follow their nose," said Hoffman. "It is very popular to use the Myler Combination bit on donkeys because it pulls on so many other pressure points."

Hoffman said if she feels it is needed for a particular donkey, she uses a stronger bit for trail riding. "I might never need to pull on it, but if my donkey should have a high-fear moment I want to be able to get control in five feet, not fifty, when on the side of a mountain."

She goes on to say that in a higher level of horsemanship, touch, release, and feel are needed to train a mule or donkey to respond lightly and softly to the bit, or any other cues for that matter. "They are smart and sensitive but have the predisposition to get heavy and pushy if you don't stay aware," Hoffman explains.

A harness is required for a driving or plowing with a donkey. Again, fit is very important. Synthetic materials are fine for work and pleasure, but a leather harness should be used when showing.

Packing equipment includes the packsaddle, panniers, harness, saddle pads, mantee, and the halter and lead. Panniers are the large boxes used to hold gear and supplies. Mantees, or manties, are tightly wrapped canvas bundles for packing odd shaped gear or gear too large to fit inside a pannier. The most common type of packsaddle is the sawbuck or crosstree. It is designed with two sidebars connected in the front and the back by crosspieces that form an X over the donkey's spine. The panniers or boxes are secured to the crosspieces. All of this equipment can be made from a variety of materials. Clean and inspect the packing equipment after every use to insure it is kept safe to use.

To increase the longevity and safety of tack and equipment, keep it clean and in good repair. Wipe off sweat and grime after every use. Nylon equipment can be cleaned with soap and water. A thorough cleaning should be done regularly. Take the tack apart and clean the leather carefully with saddle soap, and then apply leather conditioner or oil. Inspect it for weak spots, tears, and broken hardware. Have repairs made before using the item again. Parts most likely to wear out are areas around the buckles. Readjust the straps so they buckle in a different place to make the tack last longer. Stitching wears out

Packsaddles.

long before the leather or nylon parts. Repair stitching with a sewing awl or have it done at a saddle shop or shoe repair shop. Keep tack in a clean, dry place to prevent mold and mildew, and in an area that is inaccessible to rats, mice, and puppies, which are likely to chew on the leather.

Being well prepared before bringing the new donkey home will help assure donkey and owner will be well on their way to a long and happy relationship.

CHAPTER FIVE

ACQUIRING A DONKEY

FIRST-TIME OWNERS LOOKING FOR A SUITABLE DONKEY SHOULD first know what they want to do with the donkey: pet, show, trail ride, work, pack, drive? Donkeys come in many models, from miniature to mammoth. Questions to ask yourself are: Do I have a proper facility in which to keep a donkey? Do I have experience and knowledge needed to care for and train a donkey? Can I afford to keep a donkey? Keep in mind that donkeys are very social and will not do well alone. A donkey needs a companion, preferably another donkey, a pony, or a horse. Some may be happy with other livestock including cattle, sheep, or goats. If you do not already have a companion animal for the new donkey, consider getting two.

If you are a novice, be sure to ask an experienced donkey owner to help in your quest to find the right donkey. Have an experienced mentor ride, pack, or drive the donkey, depending on the purpose of the donkey. When that goes well, try it out yourself. It is even a good idea to go back a few days later and test the donkey again. The key is not to be in a hurry and not to fall in love with the first donkey you find. Once you have decided on the right donkey have a pre-purchase vet check done, and have a farrier to check out its feet. The seller is required to provide a current negative Coggins test, a blood test used to detect equine infectious anemia.

Donkey prices can vary from $75 to $1,500 or more. Where you are located, the age, type of donkey, and the amount of training it has had will all factor into the price.

Private sales are ideal when the seller is someone you know and trust.

Private sales are often ideal ways to find a first donkey, especially when the seller is someone you know and trust, or if you have some equine background. Rachel Karneffel and her husband own Wise Ass Acres in Colorado. She has a degree in Equine Science from Colorado State University and has a lifelong relationship with horses, particularly hunter-jumpers.

Karneffel relates her story of how she found her first donkey. "I had had mules because a friend of mine let me ride hers once and got me hooked. I am a lifelong horsewoman. When I sold my last mule, I needed a companion for my draft mare. I asked on Craigslist if anyone had an elderly donkey who might enjoy living with my mare. I got a response almost immediately from a local couple who said they had a two-year-old large donkey that had tried to kill a goat, and they needed him to go to a new home. When I met Charlie I immediately fell in love with his fractious personality. I took him, and he was one of the best gifts I ever received. Not only did he and my mare get along, but Charlie started growing and growing, so I started training him to pack in preparation for riding. I ponied him off of my mare, and he went everywhere with us. And now that my mare has crossed over, Charlie is what remains of her for me; he is my steadiest riding donkey and soul mate. We know each other completely. We trust each other in all situations. He started it all for me. I have no more horses, only donkeys!"

Adopting a donkey from one of several agencies in the United States, Canada, and other countries is another way of acquiring a donkey. These donkeys have been surrendered by previous owners for various reasons from economics to behavior problems. Some have been rescued from negligent homes or were feral donkeys. There will be an adoption fee, so these are not free donkeys. The agency usually retains the title to the donkey. They will inspect the facility of the donkey's new home and reserve the right to visit and check on the donkey at any time. The donkey cannot be moved to a new location without approval and cannot be used for breeding. In many instances, if it doesn't work out, the donkey can be returned to the agency and exchanged for another.

The Bureau of Land Management (BLM) has an adoption program designed to keep America's wild burro population under control. The minimum adoption fee is $125. While this might seem an economical way to acquire a donkey, keep in mind that most of these donkeys are not used to human contact and will present quite a challenge to unexperienced caretakers. Before being allowed to adopt a wild burro, the prospective adopter must meet the following requirements:

Be at least eighteen years of age. (Parents or guardians may adopt a wild horse or burro and allow younger family members to care for the animal.)

Have no prior conviction for inhumane treatment of animals or for violations of the Wild Free-Roaming Horses and Burros Act.

Demonstrate that you have adequate feed, water, and facilities to provide humane care for the number of animals requested.

**The breeder knows the history of the parents as well
as the health and soundness of the donkey.**

Breeders can be excellent resources for buying a young donkey.

Show that you can provide a home for the adopted animal in the United States.

Once these requirements are established, the potential adopter fills out an application. The BLM will inspect the facility where the donkey will be housed before approving the application. One year after adoption, the BLM will send a Title Eligibility Letter, which must be signed by a veterinarian or other qualified person saying the animal has been well cared for. Once the letter is approved, the adopter is issued a Certificate of Title, making the adopter full owner of the donkey.

Breeders can be excellent resources for buying a young donkey. The breeder knows the history of the parents as well as the health and soundness of the donkey. A young donkey will require training, which will add to the expense, but starting with a clean slate can be a good thing. The donkey is less likely to have acquired bad habits that come from poor training. Expect to pay more when purchasing from a breeder.

Auctions are perhaps the riskiest way to purchase a donkey for a novice or an experienced buyer. There are usually no guarantees, and little to no reliable information on the donkey's history. Even with the auction barn's best efforts, sellers sometimes hide information about an animal's health and soundness. Reputable auction barns require a recent health certificate and by law must require a negative Coggins test on all donkeys consigned to the sale.

Some auctions offer three ways to bid, in addition to the buyer being at the sale and bidding themselves: mail-in bids, phone-in bids, and surrogate bidding, which is through another registered person at the sale. A newer high-tech innovation is online bidding at live auctions. You can bid from your home computer if it is linked up to a company that specializes in Internet broadcasting and has digital cameras at the auction focused on the donkeys in the sale arena. With live video and audio, people can bid even if they are across the country from the location of the auction. The bidder has to register and qualify to receive a buyer's number and have high-speed Internet service. With the click of a mouse bidders can place their bids. This saves the expense of traveling to sales, but it is no place for a first-time buyer without an agent who really knows the business.

The advantage to buying a donkey at auction is that they often sell for much less than one bought through other venues. Keep in mind, while auction prices often seem a bargain, you may save money in the long run by buying through a breeder, private owner, or adoption agency because you will be able to screen out training, health, and soundness problems.

Of course, there are exceptions to all of the rules, as was the case with Linda Morris.

"I saw him standing alone in a pen at a sale barn in Westminster, South Carolina; he looked so forlorn. I went there just to look, not intending to buy anything. My head said 'no,' but my heart said 'buy him.' Heart won, and I brought him home."

Morris had owned horses since she was a child but had no experience with donkeys. She was a quick study and learned all she could about caring for her standard donkey. She had him gelded and later found him a good home. Since then she has owned several other donkeys, some rescues that she has rehabilitated and rehomed. She has acquired her current herd through an experienced friend who helped her find the right matches. She finds donkeys more trustworthy than horses.

"Once they trust you, they will take care of you. At seventy-two, I find this a big plus. I don't want any surprises, or falls, in my old age," she said.

Morris said she is addicted to donkeys now, with two mammoth jennets that she rides and a gelding that, in her words, "is just a big pet that doesn't do anything except eat, sleep, and poop!"

CHAPTER SIX

HEALTH AND CARE

WE'VE ALL HEARD THE OLD ADAGE, "HEALTHY AS A HORSE." But, one might say those words fit a donkey better. Donkeys are in general hardier than horses. They can withstand climate changes better, can survive with less water, are resistant to disease, and have a longer life span. Where donkeys fail most often is in their stoicism. They tolerate pain and discomfort to a higher degree than horses. For this reason they can become very sick before their human caretakers

Donkeys enjoy being groomed.

notice anything is wrong. To assure your donkey stays healthy, follow basic good management practices, which include proper nutrition, good hygiene, preventive health care, and close observation.

NUTRITION

The first criterion in maintaining the health of the donkey is proper nutrition. The most important nutrient in the donkey's diet is clean, fresh water. Donkeys need to drink between 2.5 and 6.5 gallons of water a day, depending primarily on the weather and how much work they are doing. It is important to monitor how much the donkey is drinking each day. Water should be about 55 degrees Fahrenheit to be most palatable. During freezing weather, the ice has to be kept off the water's surface, which can be accomplished with a hammer to break the ice or by installing a livestock water heater that will keep the water above freezing temperature. When using an electric water heater, be sure the donkey cannot reach the cord or element. Take care during the summer months not to let the donkey's drinking water become stagnant. Empty the buckets or trough frequently, scrub them regularly, and clean and refill with fresh water to prevent algae growth.

Donkeys have a unique metabolism, developed from their natural desert habitat, in that they need less energy and protein in their diets than horses. Donkeys thrive on forages high in fiber. According to the paper *Review of Nutritional Management & Diseases Common to Donkeys* by Dr. Amy K. McLean and Dr. Camie R. Heleski, donkeys have a slower gastrointestinal tract time, meaning food stays in the donkey's digestive tract longer than it does in horses, so they digest more efficiently and therefore require less food than horses of similar size.

Overfeeding can lead to various metabolic diseases, including colic and founder. For donkeys kept in a paddock, quality grass hay diluted with straw can provide adequate food with the straw satisfying their grazing instinct while limiting calories. Hay should be free of mold, weeds, or any foreign objects. Donkeys kept in a pasture will not need additional feed in the summer. In fact, you may need to restrict their access to grass in the spring and summer months. This can be accomplished by dividing the pasture and rotating the donkeys on smaller tracts or by using a grazing muzzle. Supplement pasture with hay and straw in winter. Donkeys seldom need concentrated feeds or grains. Never feed supplements meant for other animals like cattle or swine. Do provide a salt and mineral block. Any changes in the donkey's diet should be made gradually. Monitor the donkey's eating habits. When a donkey goes off its feed, it is cause for concern and a veterinarian should be consulted.

To help evaluate a donkey's condition, the Donkey Sanctuary in Sidmouth, Devon, developed a body score system that is now widely used. The body score system is based on a rank of one to five with one being thin, five being obese, and three being ideal.

Quality grass hay is adequate food for most donkeys.

Some general highlights noted in the body condition scoring system are that the donkey scoring a one will have a thin neck; the shoulder bone can be felt; the bones show including ribs, spine, and hips; and the belly appears tucked. There is very little muscle cover, making it look emaciated.

The donkey with a score of two will have some muscle covering the bones and the ribs are not visible but can be felt. It has poor muscle cover on the hindquarters and the hip bones can be felt.

A score of three is ideal with good muscle development. Belly is firm with good muscle, the ribs can be felt but have a light cover of fat and muscle, and the hip bones are rounded, but can also be felt.

A score of four means the donkey is fat. The neck is thick and the shoulder is covered in an even layer of fat. Firm pressure is required to feel the ribs as well as the hindquarters.

The obese donkey scores a five with a thick crest bulging with fat, unable to feel withers or spine through the broad back, and unable to feel the hip bones. Fat deposits are often uneven and bulging.

One way to estimate a donkey's weight is to multiply the girth (the circumference of the body measuring just behind the front legs) times the length (from the point of the shoulder to the tail) times the height (from the ground to the top of the withers), and then divide by three hundred. This information will be needed when calculating dosages for dewormers and medications.

PREVENTIVE HEALTH CARE

Preventing disease and health problems, in addition to proper nutrition, good hygiene, close observation, and a safe environment, must also include regular vaccinations and a regular deworming program. Part of observing your donkey includes knowing the normal ranges of its vital signs. Check your donkey's vital signs daily for a week and record the averages. Then, periodically monitor your donkey's temperature, pulse, and respiration. The normal range of temperature is

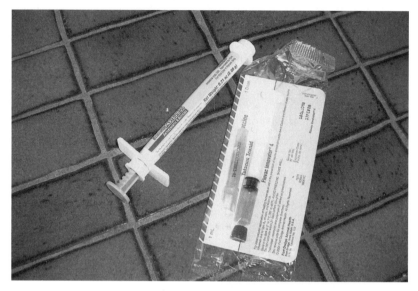

**Regular vaccinations and deworming are
important to preventive health care.**

97.2 to 100 degrees Fahrenheit; pulse is 36 to 68 beats per minute;
and respiration is 12 to 44 breaths per minute. Another way to monitor your donkey's well-being is daily grooming. While you groom
your donkey, notice its demeanor and look for abnormalities such
as wounds or sores. Clean its hooves and examine them for thrush,
stones, and signs of white line separation. Also, take note of any
lameness or touchy places that may indicate pain.

Most donkeys should be vaccinated annually against eastern and
western encephalitis, West Nile, equine influenza, rhinopneumonitis,
and rabies. Check with your veterinarian or cooperative extension
livestock agent to find out what other vaccinations are recommended
for donkeys in your area.

Equine infectious anemia (EIA) is a viral disease that infects
donkeys and other equine species. There is no cure nor vaccine to
prevent it. It is transmitted from animal to animal by biting insects. A
blood test, called the Coggins, will show if a donkey has EIA. Federal
law requires equines moving across state lines be tested. Laws vary

from state to state on the frequency of testing. Most states require that donkeys, horses, and mules be tested at least annually, especially if they are to be in contact with any other equines, and all equines entering their state must have proof of a negative Coggins. Positive animals must be euthanized or quarantined for life.

Regular grooming is important to the physical and mental health of a donkey. Most donkeys like to be groomed. It establishes the donkey-human bond through touch. Regularly grooming the donkey produces healthy skin and gives the opportunity for examining the donkey for any injuries. Applying insect repellent after grooming lessens external parasite irritations.

The donkey's environment, whether it is a stall, paddock, or pasture, should be kept clean. Picking out manure and wet bedding from the stall daily reduces bacteria and fly populations. Fumes from ammonia in wet bedding can cause respiratory disease in the donkey. The barn should allow sunlight into the stalls, as sunlight is a deterrent to the growth of bacteria. Compost manure before spreading it on a pasture that is being grazed, or spread uncomposted manure on pastures not being used for grazing. The paddocks, pastures, and stalls should be free of anything that can possibly cause injury to the donkey. Inspect the area and fences for exposed nails, sharp edges, wire, or trash. Do not store equipment such as mowers, tools, or building supplies in the same area used for the donkey's turnout.

Castration of the Male Donkey

Castration, or gelding, will result in a happier and better managed donkey. The jack has the propensity to be aggressive and harder to manage than the gelding. Unless the jack is of outstanding quality and is going to be used for breeding, life will be better for everyone concerned if he is castrated. The surgery should be done by an experienced veterinarian.

Have the donkey vaccinated for tetanus before castration. Sometimes the vet may require food to be withheld for several hours before surgery, depending on the anesthesia he will use. Provide a clean, dry area with room enough for the jack to lie down. A grassy area is ideal. Care after the surgery includes providing clean, dry turnout with a quiet companion. Some bleeding is to be expected, especially on mature donkeys. Hand trot the donkey about ten minutes at a time twice a day for about a week following the surgery to minimize swelling. Complete healing takes a few weeks. The castrated donkey should be kept separate from jennets up to six weeks after surgery to avoid an unwanted pregnancy.

Donkeys, especially miniature donkeys, need to have the spermatic cord tied during the castration procedure to prevent excessive bleeding. Donkeys tend to bleed more than horses, and some are very heavy bleeders. This should be discussed before the surgery with the veterinarian.

Signs of infection are depression, a fever, and the donkey going off its feed. Another concern is the development of a hernia, which is tissue protruding from the surgical site. Call the veterinarian immediately if you suspect either situation as they can be lethal.

DENTAL CARE

The donkey's teeth should be checked at least twice a year. Like all equines, donkeys' teeth grow continually. In the process of eating, the teeth wear down, but depending on their diet the teeth sometimes wear unevenly, causing sharp edges to form. The sharp edges are painful, especially while the donkey is eating. The veterinarian or equine dentist can remedy this problem by floating, or filing, the sharp edges. It is far better to take care of these problems when they are minor than waiting until the donkey is in distress. Signs of tooth problems include difficulty eating, weight loss, excessive salivation, and bad breath.

Hoof Care

Proper hoof care includes cleaning the donkey's hooves regularly and keeping the donkey's environment clean and dry. The donkey's hooves are normally smaller than those of the horse, with a steeper angle. The shape of the bottom of the hoof is more oblong, and the hoof wall has an even thickness all the way around. The sole is also thicker than the sole of a horse's hoof. This generally makes the donkey's hooves stronger than those of the horse. For these reasons donkeys often do not need to be shod. The exception is when planning to ride in rough or rocky terrain that is not normal footing for the donkey. In that case shoes will help prevent bruising or breakage of the hoof.

The hoof should be trimmed every six to ten weeks, preferably by a farrier with donkey experience. Note that it is not the job of the farrier to train the donkey to have its feet handled. The owner should handle the donkey's feet frequently, teaching it to lift its foot willingly for cleaning.

A healthy hoof is first gained through good nutrition and can be recognized by a natural gloss on its surface. The frog, a triangular pad on the bottom of the foot, should be the consistency of a pencil eraser when it is healthy. There should be no separation between the wall and the sole of the foot, as this opens the door to bacteria reaching the sensitive part of the foot.

Thrush is a common hoof disease, detected by a strong, foul odor, and black discharge in the area of the frog. It is caused by an anaerobic bacteria, meaning it doesn't survive when exposed to air. The best line of defense is prevention, which can be accomplished by regular cleaning and exposing the sole to air. A hoof that does get thrush can be treated with a variety of remedies that can be purchased over the counter anywhere that sells horse supplies. These products usually contain gentian violet, an antiseptic, and copper naphthenate, a chemical element that acts as a fungicide.

The donkey's hooves should be trimmed and/
or shod every six to ten weeks.

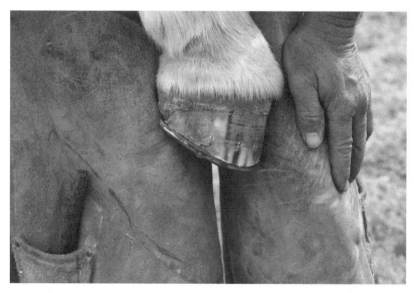

Shoes may be needed when riding on rocky terrain.

Founder is caused by laminitis, or inflammation of the lamina, the connective tissue that holds the hoof wall to the foot. Many things can cause this inflammation including concussion, overeating, obesity, or any systemic disease that causes a high fever. In donkeys it is often due to injury or abscess. Founder in the most severe cases can cause complete separation of the hoof wall allowing the coffin bone to rotate and drop down to or through the sole of the foot.

The usual signs of founder are heat in the hoof, anxiety, trembling, and increased respiration, all due to the severe pain this condition causes. Because donkeys often do not show those normal signs of pain, the condition can reach advanced stages before the owner notices. A veterinarian should be called at once if founder is suspected. While waiting for the vet, stand the donkey's affected feet in ice water to reduce the inflammation. The treatment involves drugs to reduce the inflammation, removing the cause of the condition, and corrective trimming by a qualified farrier.

White line disease occurs when there is a separation of the hoof wall and sand, gravel, or other debris works its way up into the white line. A painful abscess can form, which causes lameness. Seedy toe occurs when the foreign material and infection work their way into the hoof wall lamina tissue, which then becomes crumbly. This causes deterioration of the wall and breakage.

White line disease and seedy toe can occur for several reasons, but an actual cause is really not known. Some possible causes are wet and dirty stalls and paddocks, poor nutrition, laminitis or founder, overgrown hooves, bacteria and/or fungi in the soil, and old age. The donkey's white line is the weakest part of its hoof; it is three to four times thicker than that of a horse. This makes donkeys more susceptible to white line disease than horses.

Abscesses can be a secondary condition of laminitis or founder or can be caused by a bruise or a grain of sand or other foreign object working its way from the white line to the coronet band, where it

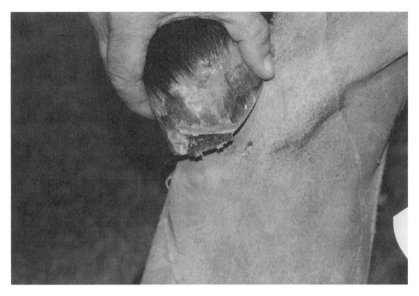

Trimming away the affected tissue of white line disease.

then ruptures. Once it ruptures the pain will subside. A farrier may be able to lance the abscess. If not, a poultice or soaking in Epsom salts will help. Once the rupture occurs, the wound should be packed with an antibacterial agent and the hole kept packed until it heals.

White line and seedy toe require diligent care that in some cases includes trimming away the affected tissue and hoof reconstruction. Follow up with an antibacterial or antifungal product like iodine, bleach, hydrogen peroxide, copper sulfate, or one of several commercial hoof disinfectants. Keep the hoof dry and exposed to air while it heals. Be sure the donkey's stall and turn out is dry and clean during its recovery time. It can take a year for new growth to replace the area that was cut out. Shoes may be prescribed to protect the hoof during the regrowth period. The amount of damage determines how long it will take until the donkey is sound again.

DONKEY AILMENTS

Besnoitiosis is a disease caused by the cyst-forming protozoan parasites, *besnoitia*. The disease is most commonly found in the subtropics of Africa and Asia but has occurred more frequently in America in recent years. Signs that the donkey is infected with the parasite include tiny cysts on the skin of the nostrils, ears, face, the eye surface, body, and inside the throat. They sometimes infect the internal organs. Some donkeys show no ill effects from the disease. A skin biopsy can distinguish besnoitiosis from other skin ailments.

Sally Anne L. Ness, DVM, DACVIM of the College of Veterinary Medicine at Cornell University, who has participated in research on the disease, writes in an e-mail interview, "There are still no effective treatments for besnoitiosis in donkeys. There is a blood test available that works quite well (we did the research on the blood test here at Cornell), but it is not yet commercially available. I hope that Cornell will soon offer it to veterinarians and donkey owners. As far as I know, no vaccines are being developed for donkeys at this time. This is most likely due to the relatively small number of infected donkeys here in the US compared to cattle in Europe, where this disease is a very big problem."

Colic is a general term referring to abdominal pain. It can have several causes. Because of the donkey's stoicism, colic can reach severe stages before the caretaker notices a problem. It is important to monitor the donkey's vital signs and behavior to be alert to changes that may indicate illness. Some signs of colic are depression or dullness in the donkey's demeanor, elevated heart and respiration, and dehydration. A veterinarian should be called as soon as colic is suspected. Treatment may include pain relief, IV fluids, medications to get the gut moving, and in the most severe cases surgery may be required. Prevention includes maintaining a proper diet, sufficient water intake, and regular exercise.

Equine insulin resistance (IR) is a metabolic disease that can be a problem especially for miniature, small, and aged donkeys. Overfeeding and obesity are key factors in the disease. The condition can lead to laminitis and hyperlipidemia. Insulin resistance occurs when tissues no longer respond to insulin, and therefore blood glucose concentrations are poorly regulated. Blood glucose levels can remain elevated, particularly after a meal rich in starch and sugar.

IR can be diagnosed by a veterinarian with blood tests. While there is no cure for insulin resistance, good management practices will help the donkey live well. Reduce calorie intake, especially carbohydrates. Feed moderate-quality grass hay—no legumes. Some research shows that soaking hay in warm water before feeding reduces the carbohydrate content by 40 percent. Warm-season grasses are lower in carbohydrates than cool-season grasses. Do not feed grain and do not give the donkey treats like candy and cookies, or even carrots and apples, which are high in sugar even though they seem like healthy food. Longeing, ground driving, and walking are good ways to increase the donkey's daily exercise.

Glanders is not a common disease for donkeys or other equines in the United States. Until recently, there had not been a case since 1942. But in March 2015, five donkeys strayed from Mexico into Texas where they were put in quarantine and tested for various diseases including glanders. One of the donkeys tested positive for this highly contagious and fatal disease. Glanders is zoonotic, meaning it can be passed to other animals and humans. Signs include respiratory infection, yellow-green nasal discharge, ulcers on the nose, enlarged lymph nodes, and nodules on the skin. Animals testing positive are euthanized. All contaminated bedding and food is burned or buried. Some sources say it can take up to a year for the area where the infected animal was kept to be free of the bacteria that causes the disease.

Hyperlipidemia is a metabolic disorder caused by increase in lipid concentrates in the blood. It is caused by several factors including overfeeding or decreasing food too rapidly to get the donkey to lose weight, stress, pregnancy, and insulin resistance. The mortality rate is 60 to 80 percent, with liver or kidney failure the cause of death in most cases. Signs include depression, not eating, head pressing, diarrhea, colic, seizures, jaundice, and gray or white tongue. The faster treatment is given, the better the outcome. Treatment includes dealing with the cause, IV fluids, and nutritional management.

Sarcoid is a type of skin cancer prevalent in donkeys. The cause is unknown, but there is some speculation that it is caused by viruses. It can appear anywhere on the body. Tumors can grow and multiply quickly, but only on the skin; they do not spread to internal organs. Treatment usually includes some method of removal, radiation, chemotherapy, or topical medicine, but is complicated and expensive. The best results occur when applied in very early stages. It is believed that sarcoid can be transmitted from equine to equine. Secondary infections are caused by rubbing and other irritations. While not usually fatal, the size and location of the tumors can render the animal useless as far as work or riding is concerned.

Strangles is a highly contagious respiratory disease caused by *Streptococcus equi*. The incubation period is up to two weeks with the first sign being a high fever followed by nasal discharge and swollen lymph glands, which can cause difficulty swallowing, hence the name strangles. The donkey will lower and extend its head and neck in an attempt to relieve the pressure of the swelling. Eventually the glands rupture and drain.

The disease is easily transmitted by direct contact, contaminated buckets and water troughs, grooming tools, and basically anything the sick donkey comes in contact with, including the handler. Serious complications can occur, causing death in a small percentage of cases. It is particularly lethal to young foals. Otherwise, the average donkey recovers with good care, although it can take months. To prevent an epidemic, isolate the infected animal from contact with any other equines. Disinfect everything the donkey has contacted. Some recommend treating with antibiotics. The antibiotic treatments must be started early and can cause side effects such as painful inflammation. Treating with antibiotics may also delay recovery and prevent immunity to the disease. This is something to discuss with your veterinarian.

There is a vaccine available that helps prevent the disease or at least lessens the severity. To prevent strangles, quarantine any new horses, mules, or donkeys entering the farm for three weeks before exposing them to other equines.

INTERNAL PARASITES

Internal parasite infestation can cause weight loss, enteritis, peritonitis, colic, and death. Donkeys are prone to the same parasites as horses and mules. A clean environment and regular deworming will protect your donkey from the ill effects of internal parasites.

Ascarids, also known as roundworms, are contracted when the donkey ingests the eggs while eating. Once the eggs reach the stomach they develop into larvae, which migrate to the liver, heart, and lungs. From the lungs they are coughed up and swallowed. In the stomach the larvae develop into egg-laying adults. The life cycle takes about three months. Adult donkeys do not have the same resistance to roundworms as adult horses.

Bot flies are another harmful parasite. The adult fly lays its eggs on the hairs of the donkey. These are swallowed when the donkey grooms itself and hatch into larvae inside the mouth, stay there about a month, then migrate to the stomach and attach to the stomach lining. There they live for up to a year, causing damage such as ulcers. They are passed out with feces, grow to the pupae stage, then

Carol Gurkin and her Mammoth donkey, Jolene.

Debbie Richardson riding her donkey in a field of sunflowers. *Photo courtesy of Shannon Hoffman*

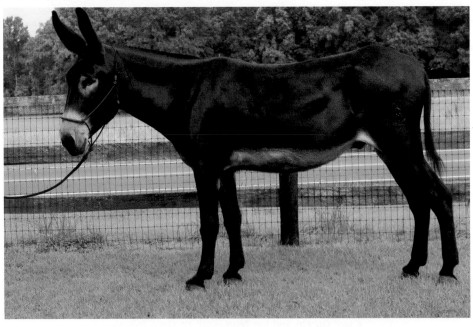

A mammoth gelding named Audie, owned by Aimee Mitchell.

Molly takes guarding the calves very seriously. Owned by Bob Radcliff.

Navarre, a Poitou, gets clipped twice a year.

Jolene ponders whether or not the flag is a threat.

Miniature ivory jenny with spotted foal owned by Renee Phillabaum.

Nothing's as cute as a miniature donkey foal. This one's owned by Renee Phillabaum.

Riders hit the trail with their surefooted companions. *Photo courtesy of Shannon Hoffman*

Watching from his run-in shed, here's a standard donkey owned by Darrell and Pat Cash.

Wee Ones White Feather in cart for Christmas, shown by Deb Mix.

to adult fly, and finally repeat the cycle. Remove bot eggs from the donkey's hair by scraping them off with sandpaper or a bot removal knife that you can buy at a tack shop.

Lungworms infect about 70 percent of all donkeys. Signs are coughing and nasal discharge. Lungworms damage the lungs extensively. Donkeys ingest the larvae while grazing. The larvae move from the digestive system to the lungs, where they develop into adult worms that can be up to four inches long. In two to three months, eggs are laid. The eggs migrate to the throat where they are swallowed and then passed out through feces. Once they reach the ground they hatch and become larvae. The cycle is repeated. While horses are not a natural host for lungworms, they can become infected when pastured with donkeys. The recommended treatment is administering ivermectin every six to eight months.

Small and large **strongyles**, also known as blood worms or red worms, are also ingested by the donkey while grazing. The eggs hatch into larvae in the intestinal tract. Some varieties settle in the liver or other organs. They can cause colic or blood vessel ruptures.

Tapeworm eggs are first ingested by tiny mites that live on the grass. The donkey ingests the mites while grazing. The eggs mature into adult tapeworms. The tapeworms attach to the intestinal wall and feed off the nutrients there. Their eggs are passed out in the horse's feces and the cycle repeats. Tapeworms cause unthriftiness in the donkey since they are depleting it of nutrients. A heavy infestation can also cause colic.

To prevent internal parasite problems in donkeys, deworm using one of many commercial products three to six times a year, rotating the products so the parasites do not develop a resistance to the chemicals in the product. Follow instructions carefully, using the correct dosage according to the donkey's weight. In addition to a regular deworming program, keep the donkey's environment clean of fecal droppings as an important deterrent to internal parasite infestation.

Cleaning stalls daily, rotating pastures, and picking up fecal matter in paddocks and pastures will help break the life cycle of most internal parasites.

EXTERNAL PARASITES

External parasites include flies, mosquitoes, ticks, and lice. These parasites carry disease, cause skin irritations, and cause mental distress in donkeys. Good sanitation and the use of insect repellents will help control external parasites. Ticks and flying parasites such as flies and gnats can be controlled with repellents.

Donkeys are more likely to be infested with lice than horses. Not only do they have a heavier coat than horses, they shed their winter coats later in the season, giving the lice more time to become established. The donkey will rub to relieve itching, causing sores, which eventually can lead to infection, anemia, and other secondary illness. Treatment usually requires a veterinarian's help. Most over-the-counter products are not effective.

Keeping the donkey's surroundings clean will go far to reduce all external parasites. Managing the pasture by not overstocking with too many animals, rotating, mowing, and harrowing the pasture will help control external parasite population.

Fortunately, donkeys are hardy animals. If attention is paid to proper feeding and practicing preventive health care, they should do well with a life expectancy of thirty to fifty years.

WHEN A DONKEY DIES

The thought of one of our donkeys dying is not one we like to consider, but whether because of sickness, accident, or old age, death is a reality we will face at some point in time. How to dispose of the carcass is an important question and one that should be researched before we are faced with the problem. Burial, cremation, or having a rendering plant pick up the carcass are some methods that are normally accepted. Most states have laws to cover the disposal of dead domestic animals. The guidelines include rules about the burial site, how much soil must cover the carcass, and reporting the location of the burial site to authorities. Donkey owners can check with their local livestock agents to learn their state's laws for dead animal disposal.

CHAPTER SEVEN

WORKING DONKEYS

DONKEYS HAVE BEEN USED TO HELP HUMANS WITH THEIR work for more than four thousand years. Today they are still used throughout the world for transportation of goods and people, farming, packing, milling, raising water, and guarding livestock from predators.

TRANSPORTATION

Transportation has been the primary use of donkeys around the world for centuries. Ninety-six percent of the donkeys in the world are in developing countries where the people depend on them for their livelihood. Donkeys are cheap and can hold up under drought conditions much better than other draft animals. China, followed by Ethiopia, Pakistan, and Mexico, has the largest number (in the millions) of working donkeys. They are used for transporting people, goods, and construction materials. Donkeys are also used for tilling farmland, milling, and to raise water from wells. In fact, in many developing countries the use of donkeys has risen because of the skyrocketing cost of fuel. People in poor countries have abandoned use of gasoline-powered vehicles and instead depend on donkey-powered carts for their transportation.

While working donkeys are not a key factor in the American economy, some are still being used for transportation in special circumstances. Donkeys in America are probably best remembered for their use by early prospectors and miners in the West, especially

Shepherds using a donkey to haul water in the Sahara desert, Tunisia, Africa. *Photo by Jacqueline Macou*

during the gold-rush days. Today in America donkeys are used to pack materials and supplies into wilderness areas not accessible by motor vehicles. Used mostly in recreational ventures, pack donkeys are used to carry supplies for backcountry camping, fishing, and hunting trips. In some cases they are also used to transport building materials and supplies to areas that are not reachable by motor vehicles. The material packed by donkeys is called dunnage. Packers generally charge according to the weight of the loads carried by the donkeys. The National Park Service and National Forest Service both have packing stations in some of their remote areas.

THE MILITARY

Donkeys and other animals are used by the military as pack animals in remote areas like mountains, deserts, and jungles. In 2004 the United States Army's John F. Kennedy Special Warfare Center and School at Fort Bragg issued a 225-page field manual titled *Special*

Forces Use of Pack Animals. The manual covers selection, care, and training of donkeys and other pack animals.

The manual describes the donkey personality: "Donkeys are cautious of changes in their environment. Donkeys have a strong sense of survival. If they deem something as dangerous, they will not do it. It is not stubbornness—it is Mother Nature, and they are smart enough to know when they cannot handle something. A handler should never lose his temper or use brute force to accomplish a task because the donkey will then fear his handler for life. Yet, with trust and confidence in their handlers, donkeys will go along with what tasks are necessary and accomplish the mission."

Soldiers receive hands-on training on handling donkeys while still in the States. Overseas, they learn to use whatever animal is available, donkeys or mules, in whatever places they find themselves in order to get their job done. Donkeys and mules are readily available in many Middle Eastern countries where they are still used as beasts of burden and for transportation.

FARMING

It is common in many countries to use donkeys for plowing, milling, and hauling. Even those in developed countries who own donkeys for recreation and pleasure sometimes put their donkeys to work in the garden or to help with other heavy work.

Ginny Freeman has used her donkeys to help plant seeds. She puts the seeds in panniers and walks with Aerial (her very first donkey) on the plowed ground, tossing the seeds to plant them. She also has used donkeys to drag logs and branches.

Heidi Dawson-Graham uses her two donkeys to pull brush and logs out of hard-to-access areas on her property. She finds that a well-made packsaddle is the best and most versatile piece of equipment, along with a good rope, when pulling with her donkeys. She makes it a point to praise them when they are working. She said,

Heidi Dawson-Graham uses her donkey to pull limbs on her ranch.
Photo courtesy of Heidi Dawson-Graham

"After the work is done they get a good grooming and a special treat, usually a little grain, for a job well done."

While these donkey owners may not have donkeys specifically for farming, they do put them to work to help with heavy chores when needed.

DONKEYS RAISED FOR FOOD

This is not what American donkey enthusiasts even want to think about, but in many parts of the world, including Africa, Asia, Italy, and China, consuming donkey meat is not unusual.

In the northern provinces of China donkey meat is especially popular. Donkeys that are no longer able to work are often destined for slaughter. They are also raised solely for meat production, and donkey meat is also imported to China from other countries. The hides are valuable not only as leather but as a gelatin product used in Chinese medicines and cosmetics.

In Italy donkey meat is a popular delicacy and served in many restaurants. The best-known Italian donkey dish is a stew called *stracotto d'asino* (donkey stew). Donkey meat is also used in cured meats like sausages and salami. A donkey breed named Furlana is bred exclusively for meat production and there are more than four hundred registered equine butchers in Italy.

DONKEY MILK

It has been found that donkey milk is an especially good substitute for those who are allergic to cow's milk. It is particularly well suited for infants and children as its properties are most similar to human breast milk. Donkeys do not produce the volume of milk cows do, and for this reason it is very expensive.

Tradition tells us that Cleopatra bathed in donkey milk, and its reputation as a skin care product continues today. Donkey milk is an ingredient still used in the manufacture of soap and other skin care products. Cosmetic companies in South Korea and in France are best known for using donkey's milk as an ingredient in their products. A few small farmers in the United States are experimenting with making donkey milk soap and other skin care products. One of those is Lisa Cohen of Fat Belly Farm in Newport, Maine.

Cohen said, "We started out with having mini donkeys as pets, and then one day we came across a video on the Internet about donkey milk cheese, and we were pretty intrigued because it is the most expensive cheese in the world. I started doing some research about the benefits of donkey milk since we were about to have a baby donkey. We were already making our goat milk soap, and thought it would be a great idea to start offering donkey milk soap after we weaned her. We saw that it was pretty popular soap in other countries, and at the time we were the only ones in the United States making it."

Donkey soap by Lisa Cohen, of Fat Belly Farm in Maine, one of a few artisans in the United States that make donkey soap.

According to Cohen, milking a donkey is pretty challenging. It must be done three or four times a day, because jennets don't have a reservoir to be able to store their milk. Her donkeys stop producing after about four months. The milk is rich in vitamins C, D, E, and A, and it contains a natural retinol, which is said to have anti-aging properties.

GUARDING LIVESTOCK

Donkeys make excellent livestock guards. Small hobby farmers and ranchers in the United States are turning to the donkey as protector of their herds of sheep, cattle, and other farm animals. One such rancher, Bob Radcliff, raises grass-fed cattle on his Lynch Creek Farm in central North Carolina. His spotted donkey, Molly, protects the young calves from predators like marauding stray dogs and coyotes. According to Radcliff, Molly will welcome people to the pasture and tolerates deer and wild turkeys, but any other animals are promptly escorted out of the pasture.

"She goes after anything on four legs that comes inside the pasture," Radcliff said.

This donkey takes guarding the calves on Lynch Creek Farm in central North Carolina seriously.

When choosing a donkey to guard livestock, it is important to know that not just any donkey will do. According to an Agri Facts paper, *Protecting Livestock with Guard Donkeys*, published by Alberta (Canada) Agriculture, Food and Rural Development, it is the natural aggressive behavior of donkeys toward predators that makes them useful for guarding livestock. Dr. Amy McLean, assistant professor and equine specialist at North Carolina State University, agrees that not all donkeys are created equal when it comes to being a guard. She said the best option is a gelded jack or a jennet. McLean notes that some people have tried using a jack that has not been castrated but found they can sometimes be very violent and even kill the lambs or calves they were intended to protect.

Some farmers and ranchers have tried putting two donkeys together out in a herd. Dr. McLean comments that sometimes that works, and sometimes it doesn't, because donkeys like having each other for a companion so much they pay little attention to the livestock.

According to the Canadian Agri Fact paper, donkeys' keen sense of hearing is a factor that aids in their guarding ability. The standard or mammoth donkeys, which are horse size, should be chosen over miniature donkeys. The larger donkeys are big enough to intimidate predators and hold their own, while the miniature donkeys will be no match for a coyote or pack of stray dogs. Donkeys that have been with livestock since they were weaned usually make better guards than those that have been kept with other donkeys.

When the guard donkey first arrives, it is advisable to keep it in an adjoining pasture with a fence between it and the livestock to see how it reacts. You want to be sure the donkey will not be aggressive, especially toward young animals, before turning them out together. The next step is to introduce the donkey to the livestock by first leading it around in the pasture with them. When you are assured they will be compatible, let the donkey out with the livestock, but be ready to remove it if it shows any aggression toward the livestock.

While this should go without saying, don't endanger a dog by turning it out into the pasture to test the donkey. If possible it is a good idea to take a new donkey on a trial basis so you can be certain it will work out.

THERAPY DONKEYS

The donkey's personality as a gentle and patient creature that loves attention makes it an ideal therapy animal. In donkey-assisted therapy the donkey acts as a mediator between the person and the therapist. The donkey has been used with children and adults with developmental disabilities as well as physical and mental diseases. Many equine-assisted therapy programs that primarily use horses also have donkeys. The clients benefit from contact and interaction with the donkey and by getting the donkey to respond to commands.

In the paper "Donkey-Assisted Rehabilitation Program for Children: A Pilot Study," researchers Paola De Rose, Elisabetta Cannas, and Patrizia Reinger Cantiello state that it is the ethological characteristics of the donkey that make it suitable in children's rehabilitation programs.

They write, "Primarily, its size, large but not too large, makes the donkey an unavoidable but not intimidating interlocutor. Thanks to its physical structure, the donkey's typical, open predisposition towards others provides a physically welcoming acceptance and thus an opportunity for contact and space sharing. When confronted with a new situation, the donkey does not run away from it but rather stops and ponders what to do; it's neither impulsive nor anxious and thus instinctively curious, hoping to make a connection with someone to fulfil its socialization need."

Kim Sullivan, of Round Rock, Texas, volunteers with her little donkey, Lewis, and her miniature horse, Rocky, through Pet Partners, which is a national organization that certifies animals to do therapy work. She works with Lewis the most because his calm and

Lewis, therapy donkey, with owner Kim Sullivan.

patient demeanor is so well suited for working indoors. Sullivan said Lewis is quite a bit smaller than Rocky, plus his little hooves fit perfectly in a set of high-top Build-A-Bear shoes, which keep him from slipping on slick floors.

They visit two facilities on a fairly regular basis. One is Rock Springs Behavioral Health Hospital, an acute care mental health hospital. Lewis and Sullivan visit with the adolescent boys and girls. She started out by just bringing Lewis to the unit and letting the kids pet him. She later brought a playground ball that Lewis rolls back and forth with the teenagers.

"Sometimes he rolls it to all the kids, and sometimes he acts the part of a 'stubborn donkey' and makes them work for it. He also enjoys doing other tricks, like smiling, ringing his bell, or shaking hands. I have been told that the kids and staff both look forward to our visits. More than one kid has dropped his tough, nothing-can-hurt-me look at least long enough to give Lewis a hug or interact with him. One boy even started crying as he gave Lewis a long hug around the neck. Lewis responded by draping his head over the boy's shoulder and hugging him back. I had never seen him do this and haven't seen him do it since then."

In another incident Sullivan tells of a newly admitted girl who sat slumped over at a table. She was the only one in the group that wouldn't look at Lewis that day. Lewis took Sullivan over to her.

"In cases like this, I am always cautious. I want to respect the patient's feelings and also make sure not to allow Lewis to put himself where he might get hurt. I checked with staff to make sure it was okay to approach her. Lewis gently laid his nose near her, touching her softly. She didn't respond to him, but I do think she appreciated him taking the time just to be with her."

The other facility where Sullivan and Lewis visit regularly is an assisted-living memory care facility. When they arrive, the staff usually has the residents sitting in a large circle so that Sullivan can bring

Lewis around to visit with each of them. She brings Lewis's ball with him on their nursing home visits, too.

"The residents love kicking the ball to him and he seems to enjoy pushing it back to them," she said.

Sullivan tells a story about one of their visits when Lewis interacted with a lady who was sitting at a table outside of the circle.

"She appeared to be in a later stage of dementia, as she wasn't aware of us or of what was going on around her. She also seemed somewhat distressed. When she didn't respond, I took Lewis around to the circle to visit some of the waiting residents. He tugged me back to the woman at the table, this time approaching her from the other side. She calmed down, relaxed, and talked with us. She even petted Lewis."

Does Lewis have some sort of natural intuition that enables him to know when a patient needs a little extra attention? Sullivan said, "I do believe he has an intuition. I have seen it happen on numerous occasions and have heard about other therapy animals doing the same. I have heard it explained that animals pick up on the subtle non-verbal communications that people typically miss. Other people say that animals have a psychic ability that we lack. For whatever reason, I do believe that he and other therapy animals have a God-given ability to see things we people miss, and also an ability to reach people in ways that a person can't."

CHAPTER EIGHT

PLEASURE DONKEYS

MOST DONKEY OWNERS IN AMERICA USE THEM FOR PERSONAL recreation and as companions, whether it be for trail riding, camping trips, or as family pets. The donkeys' personality makes them ideal pets and companion animals. They really seem to like people, and most are gentle and easy-going. Some owners say their donkeys have a definite sense of humor and can relate several funny antics of their donkeys.

TRAIL RIDING

Many trail riders prefer donkeys to horses because of their even temperament and sure-footedness. Most donkeys have three gaits: walk, trot, and canter. There are some that move in a four-beat single-foot gait, which makes for a very smooth ride. Donkeys prefer to walk, as it is their natural instinct to conserve their energy. This instinct is attributed to their desert origins, since desert temperatures are extremely hot. It is also the donkey's nature to stop and investigate rather than jump and run like a horse in the face of possible danger. These traits make the donkey a safe and pleasant mount when trail riding.

Shannon Hoffman, who trains mules and donkeys, says that most donkeys she has ridden have a smooth, rocking walk and a rough trot, but then a really soft canter.

Shannon said, "The thing I find most different is when they go down steep hills they seem to place their feet right in front of one

Many trail riders prefer donkeys to horses because of their even temperament and sure-footedness. *Photo courtesy of Shannon Hoffman*

another instead of side to side like a horse or mule, and it seems to have a straight down the hill guiding effect."

Rachel Karneffel finds donkeys much smoother to ride than horses, although she said the smoothness of the trot varies from donkey to donkey.

"I have found donkeys to be smoother rides. Because of their A-frame-shaped backs, they don't pull my hip out so far, making it easier to ride for longer in the hips and also the knees," Rachel explains.

Linda Morris is still riding at seventy years old. She said, "I find a good trail donkey is worth its weight in gold!"

Morris had ridden both horses and mules before she was given her first donkey. She noted two differences that she likes: their slow, steady walk and steady disposition. "It doesn't matter to them if the horse in front of them hauls butt up a hill. They rarely spook unless they feel threatened by something." Morris has only had that happen to her twice, both times on her newest trail-riding donkey. In both occasions the horse in front spun around and charged toward them. "Of course they feel threatened! Here's a tank of a horse charging at you—I'd run, too! But all in all, they are the safest ride I've had in the fifty-plus years I've been riding. I highly recommend them for the older generation."

PACKING AND TREKKING

Donkeys have a long history of working as pack animals and still hold this job all over the world. Donkeys are ideal for carrying camping supplies for the pleasure owner. The donkey gives the camper the ability to go farther off the beaten path and to take longer trips than if going by horseback or hiking only. The pack donkey can carry supplies for large groups camping for extended periods of time.

Donkeys walk slowly enough for their human companions to keep up comfortably. They don't complain about carrying all the gear, so taking a donkey on a long hiking trip is very handy. In Europe there are companies that hire out trekking donkeys. In fact there are more than three hundred professional donkey hirers in France, Belgium, and Switzerland. Some also provide food and lodging for treks of one day up to a week.

Rachel and Wolf Karneffel are taking their trekking a step further. The Colorado couple have planned a long journey with their donkeys throughout their state to raise awareness on two issues close to their hearts—welfare of donkeys and welfare of U.S. veterans. Wolf, after six years of service in the military, was diagnosed with post-traumatic stress disorder (PTSD). He credits his dog, Charles, and donkey, Raymond, as integral factors in his healing.

Rachel is a certified therapeutic riding instructor, so she is well aware of the human-equine bond and its healing power. She said, "This trip is about advocacy on behalf of both donkeys and veterans.

Wolf Karneffel donkey trekking with Rachel in the Colorado mountains. *Photo courtesy of Rachel Karneffel*

First, our mission is to educate and advocate about donkey behavior, donkey training, and donkey health. Second, our mission is to promote equine-assisted therapy through showing what donkeys (and all equines) can do for veterans' mental health and self-esteem."

The basic difference between trekking and packing is that in packing the humans are riding, rather than walking. Donkeys still carry the heavy loads, but another donkey, or maybe a mule or horse, serves as transportation for the humans.

PACK BURRO RACING

Pack donkey racing is a sport popular in Colorado that traces back to the mining days of the 1800s. It is said that miners came up with the idea as a contest between prospectors with their donkeys. Today the burros used in the races are usually pleasure donkeys that are also used for packing or trail riding. In 2012 the Colorado legislature designated pack burro racing as a summer heritage sport in Colorado.

The rules are governed by the Western Pack Burro Association. Donkeys are led by a handler through the course, which, depending on the race, can be a little as five miles or more than thirty miles. Burros forty inches and taller must carry a load that weighs at least thirty-three pounds. The load must include a pick, shovel, and pan. Optional, but recommended items to be packed are water, food, and clothes. If anything falls off the donkey during the race the team is disqualified, so good packing skills are important. There are strict anti-cruelty rules and donkeys must pass a vet check before starting the race. If the donkey gets loose from the handler they must go back to the point where the donkey's lead rope was dropped and restart. The race route is marked and must be followed precisely. The team reaching the finish line first is the winner.

DONKEYS AS PETS

All sizes and breeds of donkeys certainly can make good pets, but the miniature donkey is especially favored as a family pet. Some are no bigger than a large dog, making it possible for them to ride in a car and come indoors like the family dog, and some are even housebroken.

Kim Sullivan, a certified special education teacher in central Texas, and her miniature donkey, Lewis, volunteer with local animal-assisted therapy organizations in her area. Kim is training Lewis to go on command.

Sullivan said in an e-mail interview, "I noticed that Lewis naturally would 'hold it' when inside a building or in his stall. He also typically went poop after eating breakfast. Building on this, I would feed him in his stall in the morning and then lead him into the yard near a poop pile. If he didn't go, I took him back to his stall for about five minutes and took him out again and repeated. He was already clicker trained, so when he did go, I clicked and treated. Then I started pairing the verbal cue 'go poop' with taking him to a pile. He quickly got the idea."

Her next step will be getting Lewis to go on command more consistently at other times in the day. Consistency and patience are the keys to successful training.

Lewis is Sullivan's first donkey. She has been clicker training him for about five or six years to keep his mind busy. "He seems to enjoy it," she said. Sullivan has taught Lewis to push a ball with his nose (he plays "soccer" with nursing-home residents), ring a bell, paint pictures, shake pom-poms, and smile. She is working on teaching him to drop a basketball in a hoop.

When you add a donkey to your family, plan on having your funny bone tickled. Donkey owners often speak of their donkeys' sense of humor. Do donkeys know they are funny? According to

The miniature donkey is especially favored as a family pet.

some it would appear that they do take a child-like pleasure in making folks laugh.

Colleen Selby, owner of Starwish Ranch in Los Lunas, New Mexico, shared a story about her mini donkey, Fortissimo, who, resembled the "the unknown comic" once by putting his head in an empty feed bag. He put his head all the way inside and then lifted it up. The bag went all the way down to his shoulders. Selby said he just stood there moving his head from side to side while his audience laughed out loud. Colleen finally took the bag off the donkey's head and dropped the bag on the ground. Fortissimo simply nuzzled his head back into the bag and repeated his performance. "We think he enjoyed making us laugh," Selby said.

Jeanine Davis of Our Tiny Farm in Etowah, North Carolina, tells how her standard donkey, Hagar, now deceased, used to sneak up behind her adult daughter, very gently take the center belt loop on the back of her jeans in his teeth, and then quickly pull up, giving her a very effective wedgie. "He only did this to my daughter," Davis said, "It was funny each and every time."

Along with all their other attributes, donkeys appear to have a sense of humor, or maybe they just like the sound of us laughing. In either case, donkeys do make very entertaining pets, if one is ready and able to meet the responsibilities that go with donkey ownership and is in it for the long haul, remembering that the donkey's lifespan ranges from thirty to fifty years.

CHAPTER NINE

SHOWING YOUR DONKEY

SHOWING YOUR DONKEY CAN BE FUN AND A GOOD WAY TO promote your donkeys if you are a breeder. Most opportunities to show donkeys are at open shows, and mule and donkey shows. There are rules governing registered American miniature donkeys, but standard and mammoth donkeys do not have their own rule books. Instead, the American Donkey and Mule Society endorses the North American Saddle Mule Association's rule book and suggests it as their guideline for show competition for larger donkeys and saddle mules. The NASMA and National Miniature Donkey Association's rule books can be downloaded from their websites.

The North American Saddle Mule Association (NASMA) holds an annual national championship show that includes classes for donkeys. To be eligible to compete in any classes designated as "NASMA National Champion," exhibitors must be a member of NASMA and be showing a mule or donkey registered by the association. Donkeys cannot show in mule classes. Miniature donkeys are excluded from showing in NASMA shows.

When showing donkeys in open shows with horses, the group sponsoring the show will have its own set of rules, which in most cases generally follow American Quarter Horse Association rules.

PRE-SHOW PREPARATION

A show donkey should have a great looking, healthy coat, which begins with good nutrition and conditioning. A balanced diet with proper vitamins and minerals will produce a healthy-looking donkey with shiny feet and coat.

Conditioning and training should begin at least three months before a show. This will include strong exercise three to five days a week. If the donkey is in poor shape, start out slowly and work up to a full schedule. This can be accomplished by riding, longeing, driving, or a combination of the three. Train the donkey to stand square and quietly, lead freely at a walk and trot, and to turn readily to the right, away from the handler.

Grooming your donkey, cleaning your tack, and wearing neat and appropriate attire shows respect for the show and pride in your donkey. Pay attention to the details.

A full-body clip should be done a couple of weeks before the show. Before clipping, give the donkey a bath to wash away dirt and grime. This will make clipping easier and save wear and tear on the clipper blades. Doing it ahead of time will give the "clipper tracks" time to grow out so by the time of the show the donkey's coat looks smooth.

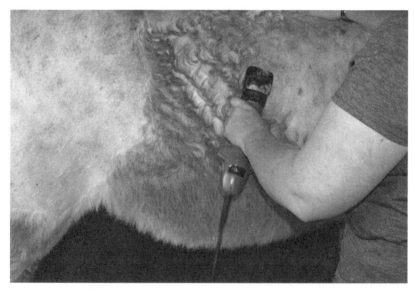

A full-body clip should be done a couple of weeks before the show.

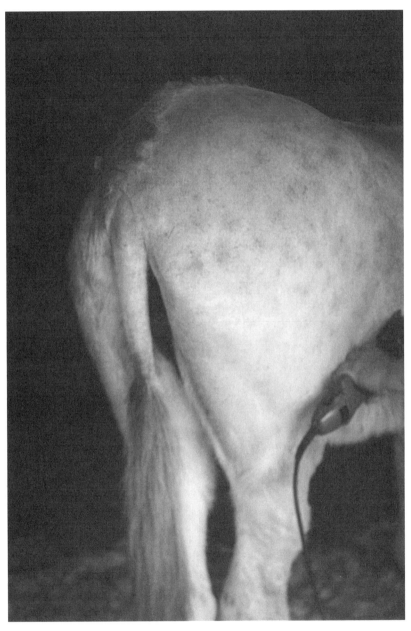

The tail is clipped, leaving a tuft at the end.

Shannon Hoffman, who owns, trains, and shows mules and donkeys in Zebulon, North Carolina, uses Orvus Paste Shampoo (Procter & Gamble), a mild detergent in a concentrated paste form that can be found in tack and farm supply stores, to wash her donkeys for a really deep clean. She clips them in the early spring, about two weeks before her first show, and again in late summer for the fall show season. She clips the whiskers, around the nose and eyes, the ears, a four to five inch bridle path, the top of the tail, and depending on how fuzzy these areas are, sometimes between the back legs, the back of the fetlock, and up the tendon.

Hoffman uses full-size body clippers for the mane, tail, and legs and small battery-powered clippers for the ears, nose, and touch-ups. She uses the body clippers to clip the hair short, usually in a square, around any brands so that observers can read the brand more easily.

Some people clip the entire head, using small clippers. Clip the ears inside and out. Put cotton in the ears to muffle the sound of the clippers. Leave a small diamond shape unclipped at the tips. Trimming the mane is a matter of preference. It may be easier to use scissors, since a quick jerk of the head might cause you to cut a gap in the mane if you use clippers. Be sure to touch up the muzzle the morning of the show since the whiskers grow over-night.

The donkey will need a bath the morning of the show. Rinse all the soap out thoroughly. Apply a hair polish or coat conditioner after the bath. Once the donkey is dry, brush it to smooth out the coat.

Hoffman uses plumber PVC glue on the lower half of the outside of the hoof to close in the nail holes, which prevents rot and keeps the shoes on tight. It is permissible to use black hoof polish on donkeys with black feet or clear polish on light-colored or striped hooves.

For a finishing touch, Shannon applies baby oil to the donkey's muzzle, around the eyes, and in the ears.

In addition to a sparkling clean donkey, be sure all tack and harness are cleaned, polished, and in good repair. Also, be sure to dress appropriately for the classes you are entering. The overall picture of a well turned-out donkey and handler can make the winning difference.

EVENTS

There are two types of classes in which to show a donkey: in-hand classes in which the donkey is led by a handler, and performance classes in which the donkey is ridden or driven. In-hand classes include halter and showmanship, costume, jumping, coon jumping, snigging, and trail classes.

In-Hand Classes

In-hand classes require a halter and lead line, which can be made of nylon or leather. The most important thing is that they be clean and in good repair. Leather halters adorned with silver trim and buckles are popular for larger shows.

Deb Mix showing in-hand. *Photo by LJ Mix*

Halter and showmanship classes are similar as far as grooming and turnout of the handler. The big difference between the two is the judging criteria. In halter classes, the judge evaluates the donkey's conformation, breed character, and overall quality. In showmanship the donkey is a prop, and the handler's ability to show the donkey is being assessed. How he or she handles the donkey, the grooming of the donkey, and the appearance of the handler are all considered. In showmanship the handler may have to execute a pattern with the donkey, which requires training and practice.

Halter classes may be broken down in several divisions, depending on the size of the show, which may include mammoths and standards, and those are broken down into jacks, jennets, and geldings.

Showmanship is usually a youth class, but some shows add classes for adult amateurs. In both halter and showmanship the donkey should be taught to lead in a straight line, both at a walk and a trot.

Wee Ones Lots of Spots, in 2013 at the Great Celebration in Shelbyville, Tennessee. Shown by Deb Mix. *Photo by LJ Mix*

It should be taught to halt, stand square, pivot on its hindquarters, trot off in a straight line from a standstill, and turn 360 degrees. Turns are always made to the right, away from the handler.

In showmanship there may be a posted pattern in which the handler puts the donkey through a routine, which includes the elements described above. Showmanship is scored 40 percent on the appearance of the donkey, which includes overall cleanliness, grooming, condition of hooves, and the halter and lead, which should be neat, clean, and in good repair. The appearance of the handler accounts for 10 percent of the score. The remaining 50 percent of the score is based on the presentation of the donkey, including leading and posing of the donkey, following the posted pattern, and alertness.

Snigging

According to the American miniature donkey rule book, snigging is an Australian word for dragging a load behind an equine. A snigging class tests how quickly and carefully a donkey and his handler can move a load through an obstacle course.

The rules go on to say, "The Donkey must wear a harness. The traces of the harness are attached to an evener which is attached to a log, and the log is dragged safely behind the Donkey. The Competitor shall ground drive behind the harnessed Donkey. The Competitor may carry a whip but it is not required. Show Management shall provide the log attached to an evener. Remember that for safety reasons cones are used, but please think of them as trees. You must be behind your Donkey when snigging. You will be disqualified if your Donkey goes around the cones while you walk on the outside of the cone."

Coon Jumping

Coon jumping has its roots in the South, where primarily mules, but sometimes donkeys, were used with dogs to hunt raccoons. The fur from the raccoon was a valuable commodity. Hunters brought along their mules or donkeys to pack out the furs. At times fences were an obstacle to the hunt. The long-eared equine can easily clear a fence as high as its own back from a standstill, so the fence did not stop the hunt. To protect his animal from injury when jumping a wire fence, the hunter simply threw his jacket across the fence and led the donkey or mule up to the fence, and it jumped over the fence. The hunter then retrieved his coat and climbed across the fence. In much the same way ranch chores like roping have become a competition at rodeos, coon jumping has become a popular contest at mule and donkey events.

The only equipment needed is a halter and lead rope, and the donkey is handled by one person, no helpers allowed. The handler must stay at the donkey's side as it is led into a ten-by-ten-foot square for small height donkeys, or twelve-by-twelve for large donkeys, and then it must jump a bar from a standstill. Contestants are allowed two tries with a sixty-second time limit. The handler is allowed to go over the bar with the donkey. Donkeys must make a clean jump and land in an upright position without knocking down the pole.

SADDLE PERFORMANCE CLASSES

Donkeys are ridden in several kinds of performance events including English and Western pleasure, gymkhana, specialty, and ranch classes. Refer to the governing rule book for specifics on tack and attire.

In Western and English pleasure classes the donkeys are ridden in the respective appropriate tack, and riders wear appropriate attire for the class. The donkeys are ridden at a walk, trot, and canter both ways of the ring and are judged on their way of going, obedience, and attitude. Again, these classes may be offered in divisions such as amateur, youth, and adult riders. Donkey classes are sometimes divided into junior donkeys five years old and under and senior donkeys six years and older.

Other specialty classes in which the donkeys are ridden are ranch riding, reined working donkey, trail class, donkey dressage, and side saddle.

In the reined working donkey class the donkey's willingness to be controlled is tested. The donkey is ridden in a required pattern and judged for smoothness, finesse, attitude, quickness, and authority in performing the various maneuvers while using controlled speed.

The trail class has at least six obstacles through which the donkey is ridden. Three mandatory obstacles are a bridge, gate, and a back-through.

SPEED EVENTS

Speed classes, also known as gymkhana classes, include barrel racing, pole bending, and the keyhole race. The rules call for Western attire and tack.

In pole bending the donkey runs the pattern around six poles. According to the rules set by NASMA the poles are twenty-one feet apart, with the first pole twenty-one feet from the starting line. The donkey may start either to the right or to the left of the first pole and then run the remainder of the pattern, turning at the end and running back through the poles. There is a five-second penalty for knocking over a pole. Failure to follow the course shall cause disqualification.

In barrel racing the donkey is ridden in a clover-leaf pattern around three barrels. At a signal from the starter, the contestant will run to barrel number 1, pass to the left of it, and complete an approximately 360-degree turn around it; then to barrel number 2, pass to the right of it, and complete a slightly more than 360-degree turn around it; then to barrel number 3, pass to the right of it, and sprint to the finish line, passing between barrels number 1 and 2. There is a five-second penalty for knocking over a barrel. Going off course results in disqualification.

In the keyhole race a keyhole is drawn on the ground with lime. The donkey is ridden into the keyhole, turned, and ridden back out. Stepping on or out of any of the lines results in disqualification.

DRIVING CLASSES

Various driving classes are also offered for donkeys. The foremost consideration is that the donkey be safely harnessed to the vehicle. Again, classes for standard and mammoth donkeys are judged according to North American Saddle Mule Association (NASMA) rules, and the National Miniature Donkey Association rule book governs miniature donkey shows.

Titan driven by Deb Mix. *Photo by LJ Mix*

In driving classes the only times two people are allowed in the vehicle are when two or more donkeys are hitched to the vehicle or when a junior exhibitor is showing. Even in these situations, any assistance by the second person is cause for disqualification.

Appointments include a whip. The thong on the whip must be long enough to reach the shoulder of the donkey farthest from the driver. No one may handle the reins, brake, or whip but the driver, nor can drivers be changed unless called for in the class description.

NASMA rules emphasize that the harness fit and be properly adjusted for the comfort of the animal. The bridle should fit snug to prevent it from catching on parts of the harness or vehicle. A throat-latch and noseband are required. Metal fittings should match and be secure. Because a donkey's head is larger than a mule's, a custom bridle may be needed to fit properly.

In choosing black or brown harness, keep in mind that black is correct for painted vehicles and natural stained wooden vehicles that are trimmed with black, whereas brown is correct if the natural wooden vehicle is trimmed with brown. Use a breast collar with a light vehicle and a full collar when pulling a heavy carriage or wagon.

When exhibiting in a driving class, one should consider the overall picture in choosing the vehicle. It should give a pleasing and balanced appearance, keeping the size and type of donkey and its way of going in mind. The vehicle should be in good repair, painted or stained as appropriate, and be in keeping with the rules.

Yelling, whistling, or otherwise using the voice in excess can be penalized by the judge. Clucks and voice commands are permitted in a normal tone. As in any class the showman should be able to control his or her animals with the least-obvious cues possible. Proper attire for driving classes consists of conservative modern clothes, Western or English. Women wearing a skirt should use a lap apron. Hats, long sleeves, and gloves are required.

The donkey must be sound, showing no sign of lameness, short-ness of wind, or visual impairment. Showmen should be sure their donkey is appropriately shod for driving.

Pleasure driving working classes are judged on overall appear-ance of a pleasant drive as one might take on a Sunday afternoon in the countryside. The donkey should show alertness, quality gaits, smooth transitions, and good manners. The class is scored 70 percent on performance, 20 percent on condition and fit of the harness and vehicle, and 10 percent on neatness of the turnout. The donkeys are shown both ways of the ring at a walk, trot, park trot, and road trot. They will also be expected to stand quietly when asked and to back. They may also be required to do a figure eight.

Pleasure driving is judged 40 percent on performance, manners, and way of going; 30 percent on condition, fit, and appropriate har-ness and vehicle; and 30 percent on the turnout. The class routine is the same as in pleasure working.

Reinsmanship is similar to equitation in riding classes. It is judged 75 percent on the handler's ability and 25 percent on the condition and turnout of the harness and vehicle. The class routine includes driving at a walk, trot, park trot, and road trot both ways of the ring and to stop, stand quietly, and to back. They may also be asked to execute a figure eight as extra work.

Obstacle driving classes require the donkey be driven through an obstacle course. In this class tie-downs and overchecks are pro-hibited. Each obstacle has a point value. The judge wants to see the donkey negotiate the obstacle course smoothly without disturbing the obstacles. The donkey should be alert and responsive to the driver's commands. There are six to eight obstacles. Four kinds of obstacles are mandatory: a back-through that consist of either two poles set a minimum of ten feet apart but adjusted properly for the larger vehicle widths; a box that is made by placing three rails, a mini-mum of fifteen feet long, on the ground to make a three-sided box; a serpentine that is a minimum of three poles at least fifteen feet apart (twenty feet for larger vehicles) around which the donkey is driven in a serpentine fashion at a walk or park trot; and a straight-and-narrow, which is a set of parallel poles one foot apart and at least twenty-five feet long in which the driver must keep one wheel between the poles for the whole length of the poles. No live animals or animal hides may be used as part of any obstacle and the driver may not dismount.

Two timed driving classes are double jeopardy and gambler's choice. In double jeopardy, each vehicle has two drivers. The first driver negotiates the donkey and vehicle through an obstacle course from start to finish, then hands the reins to the second driver who drives the course in reverse order, finish to starting line. There is a prescribed time limit, and if the team exceeds it, they are penalized five seconds. Five-second penalties are also given if the team knocks over or dislodges an obstacle and for each time the donkey breaks gait.

Wee Ones Tennessee Titan at Bedford County Fair in Tennessee, shown by Deb Mix. *Photo by LJ Mix*

In gambler's choice a course is set up and each obstacle is given a point value. The driver can choose his or her own path through their choice of obstacles, gambling that they will earn the most points for successfully finishing the course within a two-minute time limit.

Before entering a show, find out which rules will govern, since there may be some differences from one show to another. Training and practice are the keys to a good performance. While many things can affect the donkey's performance in a show that cannot be helped, the one thing you always can control is how well you and your donkey are turned out. Be sure you and your donkey are well groomed and appropriately attired, and be sure you are using the correct tack and appointments. If you don't finish in the ribbons, there is always another show. Meanwhile, have fun, make friends, and learn from your experience.

CHAPTER TEN

BREEDING

BEFORE MAKING THE DECISION TO BREED YOUR JENNET IT IS wise to think long and hard about whether to go through with it. Figure the cost versus adopting or buying another donkey. Consider that sanctuaries are full of donkeys needing homes. Remember, it will be a year from conception to birth, plus another three or more years before you can train the offspring for riding, driving, or packing. There will be veterinary costs for the jennet before and after the foal arrives, as well as the cost of feeding, hoof care, and vetting the foal until it is mature enough to use. You are making a large financial and work commitment when you decide to raise a foal.

After all the above considerations have been weighed and a lifetime commitment can be made, many will still want the experience of raising a donkey. There are also times when the decision to breed is taken out of the owner's hands, such as when the jennet is already bred when acquired, or in the case of accidental breeding.

In all planned equine breeding programs, the key to success is choosing the very best sire and dam possible. An offspring cannot be better than the genes given by its parents. There must be a clear understanding of what the breeder wants from the offspring. Does the breeder want to produce a saddle, pack, show, or work donkey? If miniature donkeys are the goal, then finding the best miniature jacks and jennets is the top criterion. It is not enough that they just be small. The parents must have good conformation and disposition in order to pass those traits to the foals.

Likewise, mammoth donkey breeders should not be fixated on size alone. The American Mammoth Jackstock Registry sets the following description in their handbook as the ideal for the registry:

The model Jack should be no less than 15 hands (60") tall. He should have good width, depth and length of body, a strong loin and full hip. The neck should be well muscled, but not excessively thick, and of proportionate length. The feet should be large and well cupped. Bone should be of good size, flat and clean. The legs should not be fine in appearance, resembling the leg of the Thoroughbred horse. The head should be well shaped and not of extreme length or thickness, tapering to a relatively fine, rounded muzzle, and be in good proportion to the body, with large wide set eyes, and well placed long, thin upright ears. The result of these combined qualities is a jack with style and substance that is well suited for Jack Stock production, as well as producing superior quality mules of any type.

Researching through donkey magazines, donkey associations' membership lists, farm visits, and donkey shows are all ways to find reputable breeders with good stock. One of the best ways to judge whether a jack produces quality donkeys is to look at offspring by that particular jack. If you plan to buy a jack and start your own program, be sure to find out if he has bred before, and if possible look at some of his offspring.

Today's high tech world gives one even more options in searching for the right donkeys to breed. Shopping online for a sire widens the horizons. Frozen semen can be shipped from anywhere in the world for artificial insemination (AI). Most equine vets are equipped to handle the insemination if the breeder does not have the knowledge and equipment required.

There are some difficulties with freezing donkey semen due to differences in the makeup of the sperm membrane. In addition, the jennet's cervix is smaller in diameter than the mare's and the cervix protrudes into the vagina, making insemination more diffi-cult. Despite these drawbacks, AI can still be done with success. The advantages to AI are that there is less chance of infection and more jennets can be bred by the same jack, and one can breed to a jack that is geographically distant from the jennet.

The jennet should also have excellent conformation and a good disposition. Breeding for color should be the last consideration, and never choose a mate for color over good conformation and dispo-sition. Size is important, but this goal is not without its problems. Miniature donkeys can have some genetic problems due to dwarfism in the small breeds. Be sure neither mate exhibits any dwarf charac-teristics, which include any number of defects ranging from minimal to severe. Some dwarf characteristics are short legs with an oversized head and body, retracted tendons, club feet, an undershot jaw or par-rot mouth, a dished face, bulging forehead, and mental retardation. A minimal dwarf usually is one with short legs, poorly aligned jaw, or other minor physical deformities.

The conception rate of the donkey is considered to be lower than that of the horse. Donkeys have an average gestation period of twelve months but that can vary from eleven to fourteen months. Donkeys are more likely to have twins than horses, but it is still fairly rare. Donkeys stay in heat for a longer period than do horses. They also tend to cycle year round, rather than going into anestrus during the winter months. Signs that jennets are in heat include mouth clapping, increased braying, allowing other jennets to mount her and mounting other jennets, frequent urination, vulva winking, and raising her tail.

BREEDING FOR MULES

When donkeys were first imported to the American colonies it was primarily for crossing with mares to produce mules. Although in very rare instances female mules have produced offspring, for all practical purposes the mule is sterile. That is because the horse and the donkey do not have matching pairs of chromosomes. All members of a species have the same number of chromosomes in a cell. The horse has sixty-four and the donkey sixty-two. The mule inherits thirty-two from the horse parent and thirty-one from the donkey, giving it sixty-three, an odd number of chromosomes, which cannot evenly divide and are therefore unable to match up to produce offspring.

One of the challenges of breeding the jack and mare is that often the jack is reluctant to service a mare. Even George Washington's early breeding experiments ran into this problem when Royal Gift, the first jack he received from the King of Spain, turned up its nose at Washington's mares. Only after a second jack was brought to Mount Vernon, and Royal Gift had some competition, were Washington's attempts at mule production a success.

Today's breeders often run into this problem, particularly if the jack has covered female donkeys prior to being introduced to mares. It is advised to introduce the novice jack to mares before he is allowed to breed jennets.

The tables can also be turned with the mare rejecting the jack. For these reasons pasture breeding is ill advised, with studies showing a less than 40 percent success rate. There is also a risk of injury to the jack by an unreceptive mare. Most mule breeding farms use either hand breeding or artificial breeding.

The jack is said to give his offspring long ears, his voice, sure-footedness, and hardiness. The mare gives the mule a more horse-like head and eye shape, size, body build, and disposition.

The mare should have excellent conformation. A prominent wither on the mare is important, since the donkey lacks this attribute, and good withers are necessary to hold a saddle in place. This is also important if the mule will be a pack animal. The mare should have a pleasing head and long neck. Stay away from mares with such flaws as a Roman nose, long back, crooked legs, or unbalanced build. These flaws are very likely to show up in the mule. You want a nice meld of the two animals, with neither dominating the other. While there are no guarantees even with the best sire and dam, it certainly increases the likelihood of getting a high-quality mule when you choose high-quality parents.

Breeding a jennet to a stallion produces a hinny. Some sources say hinnies are less popular than mules because they are more horse-like, smaller, and less hardy. But Cynthia Attar, author of *The Mule Companion*, and Dr. Amy K. McLean, director of international market development at the American Quarter Horse Association and whose family owns Sowhatchet Mule Farm in Georgia, both say that today's hinnies look pretty much like mules. Still, hinnies are not as common as mules.

CARE OF THE PREGNANT JENNET

The pregnant jennet's care includes conditioning, good nutrition, and all of the preventive health care that should be offered any equine. She should be up to date on all vaccinations and have booster injections thirty days before her due date. These antibodies will be passed on to the foal when it drinks the colostrum immediately after birth. Parasite control is also very important in the pregnant jennet. This affects the health of both the jennet and the fetus.

It is important to have a good relationship with an equine or large animal veterinarian. This should start with a pre-breeding checkup to be sure the jennet is breeding sound. If your jennet was already pregnant when you got her, she should have a vet examine her as soon as possible. The exam will help estimate how far along she is in the pregnancy, as well as evaluate her overall well-being and bring her up to date on vaccinations.

Jennets should receive equine rhinopneumonitis vaccinations at five, seven, and nine months of the pregnancy. While not serious in most horses, rhino can cause the pregnant mare to abort.

Exercise is another key element in maintaining all-around good health for the jennet. Light riding or ground driving and plenty of turnout space for free exercise will benefit the jennet during her pregnancy. Discontinue hard work the last four months of the pregnancy.

Feeding the pregnant jennet does not change dramatically until the last quarter of pregnancy, unless the jennet is thin. During the last quarter the amount of food may need to be increased and a calcium/phosphorous supplement added. Continue this increase for as long as the jennet is producing milk and nursing the foal.

A clean living environment is extremely necessary to the jennet and foal's well-being. The ideal situation is a well-managed pasture. In fact, this is the best place for a jennet to give birth. When this is not possible and the jennet is kept in a paddock or stall, those quarters should be cleaned daily.

If at any time during her pregnancy the jennet seems sick or is losing weight, call a veterinarian.

PARTURITION

As the foaling date approaches, the jennet owner or breeding manager will look for certain signs to signal the start of the birth process. Normally the first sign that her time is getting near is the filling out of the udder. This usually occurs around thirty days before birth. The teats fill out, a wax-like bead forms on the tips, and they may drip milk two to four days before birth.

The vulva becomes soft and loose the last two weeks of pregnancy. Then about one week before birth the muscles of the croup area become very relaxed. When the lips of the vulva swell out even with the hips, birth should occur within a few hours. As that time draws nearer, the jennet will become restless. She may seem to have colic, looking at her side, lying down and getting back up, walking in circles, and frequently urinating. Immediately before birth the jennet will hold her tail to the side away from her body.

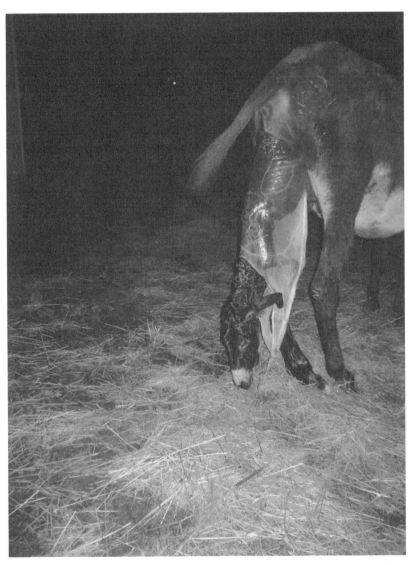

In a normal birth the two front feet appear first, with the bottoms of the hooves pointing toward the ground. *Photo by Deb Collins Kidwell*

In a normal birth the two front feet appear first with the nose right behind them. The bottoms of the hooves should point down. Any deviation from this presentation is cause for alarm, and the veterinarian should be called at once. Normal delivery should not take more than thirty minutes. If the jennet strains hard for more than twenty minutes and there is no sign of the foal appearing, or if the front hooves appear and no nose, or if only one hoof emerges, it is also time to call the vet.

CARE OF THE NEWBORN FOAL

Examine the foal and make sure the membranes are broken away from the foal's nostrils so it can breathe. Once you are sure the foal is breathing, leave it and the jennet alone to rest. The resting time allows oxygen-carrying blood to transfer from the placenta to the foal before the umbilical cord breaks.

Never cut the umbilical cord. The umbilical cord should break naturally when the jennet stands up. Leave mom and baby alone to give them time to rest and let the blood flow to the foal. Once the cord is broken, apply a 1 to 2 percent iodine solution to the stump to protect against infection.

The placenta is usually expelled within two hours after the foal is born. Call the vet if there is delay in passing the placenta. If it is not expelled within four hours, infection can occur and cause serious conditions such as founder, colic, or septicemia. Once the placenta has been expelled, examine it to be sure it is intact since any part of it left inside the jennet can still lead to infectious complications.

The first milk or colostrum contains antibodies important to the foal's immunity against diseases. This colostrum level is at its highest within the first twelve hours of birth. The newborn should be up nursing within the first hour to get full benefit from the antibodies in the colostrum. The foal cannot absorb these life-saving antibodies after it is twenty-four hours old. It is wise to have a vet examine the foal to be sure it is breathing normally, and all is well with it and the jennet.

It is also important that the foal pass the meconium within the twelve to twenty-four hours after birth. This first bowel movement is usually passed as the foal stands up to nurse. A veterinarian may need to give the foal an enema if it strains without results.

It is important that the jennet and foal be housed in a safe environment. The foaling stall should provide room for the jennet to move around without stepping on the foal and should be clean and dry. Turnout paddocks or pastures should have adequate fencing, be free of obstacles that can cause injury to the jennet or foal, and have good footing. Foals are sensitive to the cold and wet. Be sure they have protection from the elements for at least their first two weeks to avoid getting pneumonia, which can be fatal.

Foals can be fed their own ration using a creep feeder, a special foal feeder that has bars or a small hole large enough for the foal to

Foals will nibble at their dam's food within a few days of birth.

access the feed but too small for larger donkeys to reach. A creep feeder can be as simple as a board secured across a corner of the paddock, high enough for the foal to walk under to enter the corner, and situated so the dam cannot reach the feed bucket. Of course, the foal will still be getting most of its nutrition from nursing.

Scours is a common type of diarrhea in foals that usually occurs when they are eight to twelve days old. It is caused by intestinal adjustment to the digestion of food. It usually corrects itself in one or two days. Diarrhea caused by internal parasites, stress, or bacterial infection can be deadly. Care should be taken that other animals do not cause the little donkeys to run excessively, since too much exercise and separation from the dam can cause stress. Deworm the foal regularly until it is one year old, and keep its environment clean.

Navel ill, also called joint ill, shigellosis, or sleepy foal disease, is a deadly disease. It is caused by bacterial infection that enters the foal through the navel stump, which is why it is important to apply the iodine solution as soon as possible after the umbilical cord breaks. Sometimes the foal is infected through the placenta before birth. Symptoms include depression, fever, not nursing, and swollen joints. In most cases the foal will die. Good hygiene is an important preventive measure, so keep the stall clean and free of flies. If a jennet has had a previous foal with navel ill, it is possible the present foal contracted the disease before birth and the jennet should not be bred again.

If the mare was not vaccinated one month prior to foaling or if the foal did not receive adequate colostrum, tetanus antitoxin should be given at birth. Vaccination for tetanus, flu, eastern and western encephalomyelitis, and rhinopneumonitis should be given at three months, and boosters at four months. Follow the advice of your veterinarian for any other recommended vaccinations. Begin a deworming program when the foal is four to six weeks old.

Gentling the foal can begin immediately after birth. Towel it dry, especially if the weather is cool. Let the foal learn that humans are harmless by touching, scratching, and speaking to it. Then let the foal rest and explore its new world.

In a few days you can slip a halter on and off several times, run your hands down the foal's legs, and begin to pick up its feet. You can halter the foal in the stall and lead it around. Guide it around in the stall with one arm steadying the front at the chest and your other arm at its behind, giving a little push to get it moving. When the foal gets the hang of being led, go outside in an enclosed area with a helper leading the jennet, and follow with the haltered foal. Don't leave a halter on either the jennet or foal when you turn them loose as the foal might get a hoof caught in it while rearing and playing. Use a soft lead rope that is long enough to loop around the foal's behind and back to the front so as you step forward the rope gives the foal a little tug along. Practice over the early days and weeks until the foal can be led without the butt rope and then without its

Jennet and her foal.

mother. Eventually teach the foal to stand tied, and practice leading it over poles and through water. Expose it to as much as possible. All of this early training makes life so much easier for the foal, especially when it needs the attention of the vet or farrier.

WEANING THE FOAL

The donkey foal can be weaned as early as four to six months old if it is eating well by then. The easiest way to wean the foal is for it to have a buddy, whether another foal, a gentle old gelding, or even a goat. Separate the jennet and foal so they cannot see or hear each other if possible. Some breeders use a gradual weaning method, separating the jennet and foal with a sturdy fence so that the foal can stand side by side with the jennet but not reach her to nurse.

Weaning usually only takes about a week or two.

CHAPTER ELEVEN

TRAINING A DONKEY

IF YOU HAVE ACQUIRED A YOUNG DONKEY OR FOAL, OR RES-
cued one that has not been trained, you have two choices: hire a
trainer or do it yourself. If you are going to hire a trainer, be sure it
is someone experienced in training donkeys. A horse trainer that has
not worked with donkeys may not understand that there are some
differences to the approach.

An informal poll taken through several online social media
donkey groups revealed donkey owners and trainers agreed on one
important factor in donkey training: that it requires patience. That is
of course a necessary trait in training any animal. The point they were
making is that donkeys don't think like a horse. Therefore, they react
and behave differently. While the things we want to teach to a donkey are the same things we teach a horse, we may have to approach
it in different ways.

Those who have observed both horses and donkeys in their wild
and natural habitat point out basic behavioral differences between
the two. Horse rely on staying together in herds with a stallion and
his harem of several mares and their offspring. Speed is their main
defense. When they are threatened, they run away.

Wild donkeys hang out in a looser pattern of five or fewer, with
only the females and their recent offspring having a lasting bound.
Adult males are often solitary. Their color and markings enable them
to blend into their environment. When something threatens the
donkey he first stops and sizes up the situation to determine if it is
a real danger or not. If push comes to shove, the donkey will fight

off its aggressor. So, when we think a donkey is being balky, it is in reality sensing danger and is stopping to figure it out and decide how to proceed. So, rather than reacting with mob hysteria like a horse, donkeys think more independently.

Another characteristic of the donkey that affects the approach to training is its penchant to lean into pressure. They aren't being pushy so much as showing acceptance or being social, as that is what donkeys do with each other. Also, donkeys don't rush into things. The concepts of moving away from pressure and moving forward that we teach our horses don't work the same way with donkeys. Trying to get a donkey to move forward with the crack of a longe whip will more than likely cause him to stop. He is responding the way a donkey responds to potential danger. When a donkey balks the best thing to do is be patient and give him time to decide if it is safe to move on. You may even have to show him it is safe by either leading another donkey ahead, having a helper show him, or by going forward yourself.

Teaching the donkey to move forward starts from the ground.

What donkeys do respond well to is positive reinforcement. Some trainers have had great success with clicker training donkeys. Clicker training is a type of positive-reinforcement training that involves waiting for the donkey to do a desired action (take a step forward, for example) clicking a clicker (as soon as he takes one step forward), and then immediately giving the donkey a treat. The donkey quickly reasons that if he takes a step forward he will get a treat. It is called "shaping" when the donkey does a small part (takes a step) of the larger goal (moving forward freely when asked). The trainer keeps building or shaping the behavior by letting the donkey figure out the goal (to go forward freely) one step at a time. Clicker training only works if the handler is consistent and gets the timing right. A voice cue can replace a clicker, which can sometimes be unwieldy when you also have the donkey's lead rope in hand.

Rewarding donkeys even with a good neck or butt scratch when they've done a job well can often be as effective as giving treats. Eventually the donkey will respond to the cue and will not have to be rewarded every time. Trainer Shannon Hoffman had this to say about working with donkeys: "Praise, lots of praise, they truly appreciate honest praise and being made a big deal of. It only makes them want to be with you and want to try harder for you!"

Hoffman's theory of praise and reward is echoed by most donkey trainers, along with staying calm. Donkeys respond well to a relaxed and calm voice. Don't yell at a donkey or he'll think "danger!" and stop to assess the situation rather than move forward.

Donkeys have a keen sense of curiosity, which can be used to the handler's advantage. This works well with babies or donkeys that for various reasons are not used to people. Just kneeling in the corner of their stall or paddock and waiting for the donkey to approach and sniff you over until he is close enough for you to give him a little scratch or a handful of hay will usually win him over.

Haltering, leading, and ground driving are lessons to teach the donkey long before riding or putting weight of any kind on its back,

Expose your donkey to as many new situations as possible.

which should not be done before it is at least three years old. The donkey will need to learn to turn, stop, and back up on cue. Be sure to vary the training sessions because donkeys are easily bored. Work in a safe space, starting with haltering and leading in the stall, if the donkey doesn't have basic ground training. Then move to a round pen or paddock. Once the donkey is comfortable with you and doing well, move outside, leading to new and interesting places.

Ground driving involves working the donkey in harness, teaching it to move forward while walking behind it, guiding with the reins. You can teach the donkey to turn, stop, and back with voice cues. Having an assistant be at the donkey's head when introducing it to ground driving is helpful. The assistant can keep the donkey under control so that it doesn't get entangled in the reins, and encourage it to move forward. Once the donkey understands what is being asked of it the helper can move away.

Once this ground work (leading, tying, and ground driving) has been established, and once the donkey is mature enough to bear

Ground driving. *Photo courtesy of Ginny Freeman*

weight, it is seldom a problem to acclimate it to saddle or harness. It already knows to move forward, stop, turn, and back. You've exposed it to all manner of outside stimuli including sights, sounds, and smells. Give it a little time to get used to balancing with weight on its back, and you will soon be riding or driving.

Deb Collins Kidwell of Lake Nowhere Mule and Donkey Farm in Tennessee believes all donkeys must be trained the way horses should be trained—with patience. She starts training at birth, getting the foal used to touch, the halter, and its feet being picked up. By the time the foal is a week old, it is perfectly comfortable being handled.

Donkey owners have also observed that donkeys learn by watching other donkeys, or even the humans around them. Nancy Warrick Kerson has a favorite donkey-training story that illustrates the donkey's mind. "The first time I took my two new BLM burros on a walk to the neighboring property, we came to the storm grate that had to be crossed. Of course they balked. So I just stood with them calmly, petted them, put my arms around one's neck and softly said, 'Do you really think I would ask you to do something that isn't safe?

I wouldn't. It's safe.' At which time they both proceeded to walk across the storm grate. Did they understand my words? Unlikely. But they did understand my meaning."

Kerson shares another story that illustrated how donkeys learn by watching others. "One time my son and his friends were building a bike ramp, so they could go barreling down the hill, onto the ramp, and launch themselves in the air, so they could do bike tricks. Bert Burro watched them all afternoon. Then when they took a break, he went straight to the top of the hill, ran down it, and up the ramp. Thankfully he reconsidered before launching himself into the air. But I was amazed that he fully understood what the boys had been doing and was able to imitate them—and also use better sense than they had."

Giselle Louise Forrester, in Carmarthen, Wales, shares that one of her donkeys tries to sweep with the broom in his mouth after having seen her do it so many times, and takes hold of the other donkey's lead rope to lead him around.

Heidi Dawson-Graham at Buck's Run Ranch in Zenia, California, gives this advice about training donkeys: "Go slowly and pay attention to what the donkey is doing and work with them not against them. It may take all day to get them to put one hoof on a tarp, but they did it and it will be easier the next time. Carrots are your friend."

Dawson-Graham started training donkeys when she was nine or ten years old. She grew up on a large cattle ranch and always had horses around. Her father also had three teams of mules that he used for logging. She remembers coming home from school one day and seeing a strange stock trailer in the barnyard.

"Dad told me to run down and unload it before I did my chores. Inside were two scared wild donkeys. Back then they would run them into holding pens, auction them off, and then run them up a chute into your stock trailer. No handling or gentling beforehand. I got pretty banged up getting those two out of the trailer and into the round pen."

Her dad told her that if she could gentle them by summer break, they would keep them. Jack and Jill became her first donkey encounters. She says she made a few mistakes in their training, such as working them as a team not individually, which resulted in the two becoming inseparable. But, in the end, her efforts turned out well.

"Those two lived out their life on the ranch, taking care of any weanling or orphaned calves, as well as packing me and my little brother around the ranch," she said.

Dawson-Graham grew up on the ranch and worked primarily with problem horses. "You know, the ones that run off with their rider or like to kick people," she explained.

Sometimes Dawson-Graham was called on to "doctor" someone's donkey that had gotten hurt or gentle one for a client, but she didn't have a donkey herself again until 2010, when she got Boris and Natasha. She has used her donkeys for packing, pulling brush and logs, and other ranch chores. She even dresses them up in costumes for parades.

"They're my anti-depression device, pony rides for the little ones, and they keep the coyotes away," Dawson-Graham says of her multi-purpose donkeys.

"Given enough time to show them what I want them to do, they will do it. Boris even learned to pack out bear last year. I love my two. And I'm lucky they are good donkeys with good attitudes because you never know what I'll ask them to do next."

While there is nothing a donkey can't do as long as it trusts you, Dawson-Graham cautions that they have a very high sense of self-awareness and will not put up with stupidity for very long.

Understanding the donkey's five senses and how they work will go a long way to understanding how and why it reacts to outside stimuli. Probably the most misunderstood of the donkey's senses is its vision. Equine vision is quite different from human vision. Donkeys, like most grazing animals that are preyed upon, have monocular vision. With the eyes positioned on either side of the head, they see independently with each eye. This gives the donkey a wider range of vision, which is important in watching for danger and eating at the same time. They can see front, back, and sides all at once. In addition to monocular vision, donkeys have poor depth perception and are partially color-blind.

Donkeys are not fully color-blind, but have two-color, or dichromatic vision. They can see greens and blues, but not reds. So, a red apple and a green apple look pretty much the same to a donkey. The color of something doesn't mark it as worthy of note so much as if that something moves. The donkey can then switch to binocular vision and zero in on whatever moved. He does this by facing the object and using both eyes to see the one picture.

Because of the way the donkey's retina is designed, he has very poor depth perception. As far as a donkey knows, that shadow on the ground could be a deep hole. He's got to trust you to step into that shadow. The domestic donkey is asked by humans to do things that it would never do in the wild—jump a series of hurdles, pull a cart, or maneuver an obstacle course, for example. The donkey learns to trust the human trainer's judgment, rather than relying on what his sight tells him.

The donkey cannot change the shape of the eye's lens the way we can, so he has to focus by raising and lowering his head. In addition to using his head and neck for balance, it is important that the donkey have freedom to move his head so he can focus.

When you take into consideration that your donkey doesn't know how far away something is, what it is, or anything else about it, except that it *moved*, you can understand why his first instinct is to stop and look at it, and not to proceed until he is assured all is safe.

Donkeys have a keen sense of hearing, as one would expect from their large ears. Like other equines, donkeys can move their ears to discern the direction of a sound. The donkey will stop at a strange sound to decide if it means danger.

The handler can learn to tune in to the donkey's mood by observing its ears. The donkey basically turns its ears in the direction it is focused. Ears pointed forward and upright mean the donkey is watching something with interest; ears drooped down mean the donkey is relaxed; ears pinned back, donkey is irritated. Ears moving back and forth indicate the donkey is checking things out or trying to figure out where a sound is coming from. As the handler puts in more and more time with the donkey, its ears and facial expressions will tell a lot about what the donkey is thinking.

Its sense of smell is important to the donkey as a means of identifying herd- or pasture-mates and people. Donkeys give the sniff test to tell friend from stranger. By breathing into one another's nostrils in little puffs they establish relationships.

Most donkeys are very touchy-feely. They love being scratched and petted. As noted earlier, donkeys lean into pressure as a form of greeting. It can be a bit confusing to the handler when they try to

Practicing stepping over a log.

push the leaning donkey away only to have it lean in more. Donkeys have to be taught what "move away" means through training.

As you work with your donkey you will be able to tune in to what it is thinking by watching its body language. The donkey will have tuned in to your body language and voice tone probably long before you pick up on his. Ears, tail, facial expression, and body position all communicate. After all, that is what training is all about—communication. Give your donkey every reason to trust that you will not put him in harm's way, and you will enjoy a lasting relationship.

RESOURCES

ASSOCIATIONS AND GROUPS

National Miniature Donkey Association
6450 Dewey Rd.
Rome, NY 13440
www.miniaturedonkeyassociation.com/

The American Donkey and Mule Society
PO Box 1210
Lewisville, TX 75067
E-mail: lovelongears@hotmail.com
www.lovelongears.com/

American Donkey Association
Dale McCall
28371 Gimpl Hill Rd.
Eugene, OR 97402-9015
E-mail: adadonke@cmc.net
http://americandonkeyassociation.com/

American Mammoth Jackstock Registry
Linda Penman-Brotzman
PO Box 9062
Pahrump, NV 89060
(830) 330-0499
E-mail: register@amjr.us
http://amjr.us/

Canadian Donkey & Mule Association
Virginia Allen, Secretary
25766-48 Ave.
Langley, BC V4W 1J2
(604) 857-4990
www.donkeyandmule.com

The Donkey Show Site
Show dates, show results, articles about showing.
E-mail: show@thedonkeyshowsite.com
www.thedonkeyshowsite.com

Western Pack Burro Association
Brad M. Wann, Media Relations
(303) 906-2269
www.packburroracing.com

Donkey Breed Society
The Hermitage
Pootings
Edenbridge
Kent
TN8 6SD
(01732) 864414
E-mail: information@donkeybreedsociety.co.uk
http://donkeybreedsociety.co.uk/

Donkey All Breeds Society of Australia
donkeyallbreedsaustralia.org

Eeebray
Elizabeth Moore
(505) 281-5633
E-mail: allears@eeebray.com
www.eeebray.com

PRINT PUBLICATIONS

Mules and More Magazine
PO Box 460
Bland, MO 65014
(573) 646-3934
www.mulesandmore.com

The Asset
6450 Dewey Rd.
Rome, NY 13440
nmdaasset@aol.com
http://nmdaasset.com/ASSET.php

The Brayer
PO Box 1210
Lewisville, TX 75067
(972) 219-0781
E-mail: lovelongears@hotmail.com

Miniature Donkey Talk Magazine
1338 Hughes Shop Rd.
Westminster, MD 21158
(410) 875-0118
E-mail: minidonk@qis.net

FACEBOOK GROUPS

Friends of the Donkey
www.facebook.com/groups/275763069267606/

Carolina Donkey League
www.facebook.com/groups/586044561447381/

Only Donkeys
www.facebook.com/groups/688070011309593/

Glossary

Anaerobic bacteria – Bacteria that lives in an airless environment.

Anestrus – Period of time, normally the winter season, when the jennet does not come into heat; the absence of estrus.

Antibiotics – A medication that can kill harmful organisms or bacteria.

Antibodies – Immunizing agent in the body that fights disease.

Artificial insemination – A method of breeding in which the semen is collected from the stallion or jack and injected into the uterus of the mare or jennet.

Ass – *Equus africanus asinus*, also known as donkey or burro.

Auction – A sale in which the donkey is sold to the highest bidder.

Breeding sound – A state of health in which the jennet's reproductive tract is healthy, and she is overall physically able to carry a foal to full term.

Breeching – A saddle accessory that fits across the mule's hips and prevents the saddle from slipping forward when riding downhill.

Bridle – Headgear used for control when riding. Parts include the headstall, reins, and bit.

Burro – The Spanish and Portuguese word for donkey. In the American southwest it usually means a small donkey.

Canter – A three-beat controlled gait, somewhat like a gallop, but slower.

Chestnut – A natural, horny growth inside the front legs just above the knees.

Chromosomes – The part of a cell that carries the genes. They come in pairs, one from each parent.

Clicker training – A method of training that uses positive reinforcement in combination with an event marker, which is usually a clicker.

Colostrum – A mare's first milk. It contains antibodies that provide immunity against many diseases for the foal.

Concentrate – Food that is high in energy-producing carbohydrates.

Conception rate – The success of reproduction in donkeys, usually expressed as a percentage.

Conformation – The way the donkey is built.

Creep feeder – A pen or structure that is built so the foal can enter to eat without the larger animals being able to enter or access the food.

Crupper – A strap that fits around the top of the tail and attaches to the saddle.

Dam – The mother of an offspring.

Deworm – To administer a medication that kills internal parasites.

Donkey – A member of the equine family originating in northern Africa.

Donkey dressage – Dressage is a French word meaning "training." It is a high level of training that originated in the military. Today it is a competitive sport that exhibits the donkey's athletic ability through a series of maneuvers and tests.

Donkey trekking – Hiking with a donkey. The donkey is led by the hiker and used to pack supplies needed on a long hike.

Dunnage – The freight carried by pack donkeys.

Dwarfism – Having characteristics of a dwarf, which is a small and usually deformed animal.

Enteritis – Inflammation of the small intestine.

Equine infectious anemia (EIA) – A viral disease that affects the immune system. Biting insects or contaminated needles transmit EIA.

Equine influenza – One of the most common infectious diseases of the respiratory tract of equines. It is caused by the orthomyxovirus equine influenza A type 2 (A/equine 2) virus. It is very contagious, but can be prevented with annual vaccinations.

Encephalitis – Also known as sleeping sickness, a viral infection transmitted by mosquitos. A high fever is the first sign, followed by nervous system disorders. Death occurs within days. There is a vaccine available to prevent the disease.

Ethological characteristics – Behavior patterns of an animal that make up its personality.

Evener – A part of the harness used when donkeys are used in pairs; an additional crossbeam attached behind the two swingle (also known as single) trees. If one animal is stronger than the other, the connection to the implement should be attached closer to the side of the stronger animal to balance the work of animals with different strengths.

Farrier – A person trained in hoof care, including trimming the hooves and shoeing a donkey, horse, or mule.

Foal – A baby donkey, horse, or mule.

Founder – A crippling disease of the foot caused by laminitis, an inflammation of the laminae of the foot, in which the horse's coffin bone drops when the laminar bond breaks down.

Gaited donkey – A donkey that has a fourth gait in addition to the walk, trot, and canter. The fourth gait is a fast, four-beat gait also known as a single foot or donkey shuffle.

Gelding – A male donkey that has been castrated, also known as a john donkey in some areas.

Gestation – Period of time from conception to the birth of the foal.

Girth – Also called a cinch, a strap that holds the saddle in place. It fastens on one side of the saddle, passes under the belly of the donkey to the opposite side, and fastens to the other side of the saddle.

Grazing muzzle – A device that attaches to the noseband of a halter to prevent a donkey from eating too much grass. It is usually made of woven nylon strips. The donkey can still drink and it does not interfere with breathing.

Halter – Headgear for the purpose of restraining a donkey, horse, or mule. With a lead rope attached, the animal can be tied or led by the handler.

Hand – A unit for measuring the height of a donkey from the ground to the top of the withers. The unit equals four inches.

Hand breeding – Breeding with the jennet and jack under control of handlers.

Hinny – An equine hybrid resulting from crossing a male horse with a female donkey.

Immunity – Protection by antibodies against certain diseases.

In-hand class – Show class in which the handler leads, rather than rides, the donkey.

Ivermectin – A broad-spectrum antiparasitic drug in the avermectin family.

Jack – A male donkey.

Jennet or jenny – A female donkey.

Jennet jack – A jack used to breed to jennets (the female of the species) in order to produce more donkeys.

Laminitis – The inflammation of sensitive layers of tissue (laminae) inside the hoof. When it becomes chronic and the inner part of the foot detaches from the wall it is called founder.

Lipomas – Fatty tumors.

Mammoth donkey – A donkey that measures fifty-six inches or taller at the withers.

Mare – A female horse.

Meconium – The first bowel movement of the foal. The foal should pass the meconium within twenty-four hours after birth.

Miniature donkey – A donkey that measures thirty-six inches or under at maturity.

Mule – An equine hybrid resulting from crossing a male donkey with a female horse.

Mule jack – A jack used to breed mares to obtain mules.

Navel ill – Shigellosis, a septic infection in foals that is usually deadly. Also known as joint ill and sleepy foal disease. It is caused by bacteria entering through the umbilical cord.

Packsaddle – A saddle designed for supporting a load.

Packing – Using a donkey to carry loads of supplies.

Panniers – Containers or boxes that attach to the packsaddle in which to put supplies or freight.

Parrot mouth – A fault in alignment of the upper and lower teeth of a donkey in which the front edge of the top incisor teeth is farther forward that that of the lower teeth.

Park trot – Animated, square, collected, and balanced trot; extreme speed is penalized.

Parturition – The birth process.

Paso Fino – A natural lateral gait with a four-beat footfall, which provides a constant, rhythmic cadence.

Pasture breeding – Natural mating of the donkey and jennet in a pasture without restraint.

Peritonitis – An inflammation of the peritoneum, the thin membrane that lines the inner abdominal wall and covers the organs within the abdomen.

Placenta – A temporary organ that joins the dam and fetus. Oxygen and nutrients are transferred from the mother to the fetus and carbon dioxide and waste products are carried away from the fetus. It is also called afterbirth, as it is expelled from the jennet after the foal is born.

Pleasure donkey – A donkey used for personal recreation and companionship.

Rabies – RNA virus of the rhabdovirus group; hydrophobia. It is a fatal disease in mammals, transmissible through the saliva.

Ranch riding class – Ranch riding is a judged event demonstrating the abilities of the animal while working over obstacles found in everyday ranch work.

Ration – The measure of food, hay, or water given a donkey per feeding.

Reining – A judged event designed to show an animal's willingness to be guided through a pattern consisting of fast and slow circles, lead changes, sliding stops and spins.

Reinsmanship – A pleasure driving class in which entries are judged primarily on the ability and skill of the driver.

Rendering plant – A place that processes animal tissue, including dead animals, into useful products.

Retracted tendons – A genetic defect of newborn foals that affects the fetlocks and carpal joints in the front legs. The joints will appear tightly flexed and the foal will be unable to straighten its legs. It can also be caused by a bad position in the uterus. There are various treatments depending on severity.

Rhinopneumonitis – A respiratory infection. It can cause abortion in pregnant jennets and mares. Symptoms include fever, loss of appetite, and nasal discharge. Most otherwise healthy donkeys recover in about three weeks. A vaccine is available to prevent the disease, which should be given to pregnant jennets and mares.

Road trot – A balanced, ground-covering trot, without excessive speed.

Scours – Diarrhea in the foal seven to ten days old. Also called foal heat scours because it sometimes coincides with the mare's first heat cycle after giving birth.

Septicemia – Bacteria or bacterial toxins in the bloodstream. Most common cause of death in foals.

Sidesaddle – A saddle design for riding aside rather than astride. Historically women rode sidesaddle because of their long skirts, so as not to show their legs.

Sire –The male parent.

Standard donkey – Donkeys measuring over thirty-six inches and up to forty-eight inches at the withers. Most donkeys are in this category.

Studbook – A breed registry or the official record of a breed of animals whose parents are known and also registered. An open studbook accepts animals that have unregistered parents but meet the breed's standards or criteria as set forth by the breed association. A closed book means they only accept animals with parents registered with that breed's association.

Therapy donkey – A donkey used in equine-assisted therapy or other programs that use animals to treat physical and psychological health problems.

Thrush – A disease of the foot caused by anaerobic bacteria. Signs are a thick, black discharge and foul odor. Good hygiene and dry environment are the best deterrents.

Trot – A two-beat gait in which diagonal pairs of legs move together. The left front and the right hind move forward, then the right front and left hind.

Umbilical cord – Tissue that attaches the blood vessels from the placenta to the foal.

Weaning – Separating the foal from its dam so it can no longer nurse.

Weanling – A young foal that has been weaned from its mother and is no longer nursing.

Yearling – A foal that is one year old.

BIBLIOGRAPHY

BOOKS

Attar, Cynthia. *The Mule Companion.* 4th ed. British Columbia: CCB Publishing, 2009.

Clutton-Brock, Juliet. *Horse Power: A History of the Horse and Donkey in Human Society.* Cambridge, MA: Harvard University Press, 1992.

Evans, J. Warren. *Horses.* San Francisco, CA: W.H. Freeman and Company, 1981.

Smith, Donna Campbell. *The Book of Mules.* 1st ed. Guilford, CT: Lyons Press, 2009.

Svendsen, Elizabeth D. *The Professional Handbook of the Donkey.* 3rd ed. London: Whittet Books, 2000.

WEBSITES

Barnaby, Cherry. "The Famous Painting Man with a Donkey." 2012. www.toti.co.nz/he-tangata-project/sapper-horace-moore-jones/horace-moore-jones-story/the-famous-painting-man-with-a-donkey. Accessed January 6, 2015.

Burnham, Suzanne L. "Anatomical Differences of the Donkey and Mule." March 13, 2014. www.ivis.org/proceedings/aaep/2002/910102000102.pdf. Accessed June 14, 2015.

Cecchi, Francesca. "Demographic Genetics of the Endangered Amiata Donkey Breed." February 7, 2006. www.researchgate.net/publication/41393719_Demographic_genetics_of_the_endangered_Amiata_donkey_breed. Accessed May 10, 2015.

Circus Historical Society. May 3, 2002. http://www.circushistory.org/ Accessed June 1, 2015.

Cohen, Lisa. "About Our Soap." Fat Belly Farm. 2012. www
.fatbellyfarm.com/about-us/. Accessed February 24, 2015.

De Rose, Paola, Elisabetta Cannas, and Patrizia Reinger Cantiello.
"Donkey-assisted Rehabilitation Program for Children: A Pilot
Study." *PubMed*. November 4, 2011. www.iss.it/binary/neco/
cont/9.Donkey_assisted_rehabilitation_program_for_children.
De_Rose_Cannas_Reinger_Cantiello_br_.pdf. Accessed April
27, 2015.

"Donkey's Milk." Donkeys and Co. June 14, 2014. http://
donkeysandco.com/en/lechedeburra/ Accessed June 15, 2015.

Elsheikha, Hany M., Charles D. Mackenzie, Benjamin M.
Rosenthal, Judith V. Martiniuk, and Barbara Steficek.
"An Outbreak of Besnoitiosis in Miniature Donkeys."
Department of Large Animal Clinical Sciences, College of
Veterinarian Medicine. August 14, 2009. www.researchgate
.net/publication/6707022_An_outbreak_of_besnoitiosis_in_
miniature_donkeys. Accessed January 14, 2015.

Farcy, Malleus, and Droes. "Glanders." College of Veterinary
Medicine. July 2, 2013. www.cfsph.iastate.edu/Factsheets/
pdfs/glanders.pdf. Accessed April 6, 2015.

Foster, Race, and Marty Smith. "Internal Parasites Common in
Horses." Doctors Foster and Smith. www.drsfostersmith.com/
pic/article.cfm?articleid=1602. Accessed June 4, 2015.

Gosden, Lee, and Gemma Lilly. "Dental Care Information
for Owners." The Donkey Sanctuary. 2009. www
.thedonkeysanctuary.org.uk/sites/sanctuary/files/
document/142-1423234830-donkey_health_and_welfare_0
.pdf. Accessed March 29, 2015.

Knottenbelt, Derek C. "The Equine Sarcoid." IVIS. February
1, 2008. www.ivis.org/proceedings/weva/2008/
mainsession1/10.pdf?LA=1. Accessed March 29, 2015.

Larson, Erica. "Samples Sought for Donkey Besnoitiosis
    Research." *The Horse*. February 16, 2012. www.thehorse
    .com/articles/28714/samples-sought-for-donkey-besnoitiosis-
    research. Accessed March 18, 2015.

Marshall, Fiona, and Lior Weissbrod. "Introduction Domestication
    of the Donkey Influenced the Course of Development of
    Mobile Pastoral Societies in Africa and the Expansion of
    Ancient Egyptian and Sumerian Land-Based Trade Routes."
    Research Gate. Marshall, 2007; Rossel et al. 2008. www
    .researchgate.net/publication/231225965_The_consequences_
    of_women's_use_of_donkeys_for_pastoral_flexibility_Maasai_
    ethnoarchaeology

McLean, Amy. "Comparing the Physiological and Biochemical
    Parameters of Mules and Hinnies to Horses and Donkeys."
    SOAS, University of London. November 21, 2014. http://
    static1.squarespace.com/static/52f6e70ae4b09d0c250122c6/
    t/5445a26ae4b0c0bbe11f29f3/1413849706691/
    hinniesandmules_amy.pdf. Accessed March 21, 2015.

———. "Donkey Differences in Regards to Reproduction."
    American Mule Association. www.americanmuleassociation
    .org/donkey-differences-in-regards-to-reproduction. Accessed
    April 28, 2015.

McLean, Amy, and Camie R. Heleski. "Review of Nutritional
    Management & Diseases Common to Donkeys." Sowhatchet
    Mule Farm Inc. March 13, 2014. www.sowhatchetmulefarminc
    .com/articles/donkeynutrition.pdf. Accessed March 29, 2015.

Moehlman, Patricia Des Roses. "Equids: Zebras, Asses, and
    Horses: Status Survey and Conservation Action Plan." IUCN,
    International Union for Conservation of Nature. 2002.
    Accessed January 9, 2015.

"National Wild Horse and Burro Program." Bureau of Land
    Management. May 14, 2013. www.blm.gov/wo/st/en/prog/
    whbprogram.html. Accessed February 14, 2015.

Ness, Sally Anne L. "Besnoitiosis in Donkeys." *The Horse*. May
1, 2012. www.thehorse.com/articles/29113/besnoitiosis-in-
donkeys. Accessed March 18, 2015.

"North American Saddle Mule Association 2015–2016 Official
Handbook Bylaws Rules & Regulations." North American
Mule Association. April 29, 2015. www.nasma.us/RuleBook/
TENTH%20EDITION/TENTH%20EDITION.pdf. Accessed
May 3, 2015.

"Official Show Rules for the National Miniature Donkey
Association (NMDA)." The National Miniature Donkey
Association. 2011. www.nmdaasset.com/downloads/NMDA_
ShowRules.pdf. Accessed June 14, 2015.

Patton, Leah. "Healthy as a Horse, Stubborn as a Mule." *Saddle
Mule News*. April 20, 2014. www.saddlemulenews.com/
HealthyAsAHorse.htm. Accessed March 29, 2015.

Pearson, Anne, and Timothy E. Simalenga. "Harnessing and
Hitching Donkeys, Mules and Horses for Work." www
.agrobiodiversity.net/topic_network/donkey/Best_Practise/
Harness%20Hitching%20donkeys%20Oct06.pdf. Accessed June
14, 2015.

Podesia, Lynn. "Showmanship at Halter vs Halter." The Donkey
Show Site. November 11, 2011. www.thedonkeyshowsite
.com/uploads/5/3/3/6/53361531/showmanshiplynn.pdf.
Accessed April 22, 2015.

"Protecting Livestock with Guard Donkeys." Alberta Donkey and
Mule. January 24, 2010. www.albertadonkeyandmule.com/
pdfs/guard-donkeys.pdf. Accessed June 4, 2015.

Pugh, D.G. "Donkey Reproduction." American Mule Association.
2002. www.americanmuleassociation.org/donkey-reproduction.
Accessed March 29, 2015.

Purdy, Linda. "Donkeys in Africa." UMass International Donkey
Project. February 23, 2011. www.umass.edu/vasci/faculty/
purdy/DonkeysinAfrica.htm. Accessed June 14, 2015.

Purdy, Steven R. "Reproduction in Donkeys." Department of
Veterinary and Animal Sciences. June 20, 2012. http://www
.vasci.umass.edu/sites/vasci/files/reproduction_in_donkeys
.pdf. Accessed May 19, 2015.

Regan, F.H., J. Hockenhull, J. C. Pritchard, W. E. Waterman-
Pearson, and H. R. Whay. "Identifying Behavioural Differences
in Working Donkeys in Response to Analgesic Administration."
Wiley Online Library. January 20, 2015. http://onlinelibrary
.wiley.com/doi/10.1111/evj.12356/full. Accessed January 22,
2015.

Sellnow, Les. "Health Concerns of Mules and Donkeys."
The Horse. November 1, 1998. www.thehorse.com/
articles/10538/health-concerns-of-mules-and-donkeys.
Accessed March 24, 2015.

"Special Forces Use of Pack Animals, Field Manual." Field Manual.
May 5, 2014. http://quikmaneuvers.com/files/Special_
Forces_Use_of_Pack_Animals_ToC.pdf. Accessed June 14,
2015.

Svendsen, Elizabeth D. "A Guide to Worming Your Donkey." The
Donkey Sanctuary. 2013. www.thedonkeysanctuary.org.uk/
sites/sanctuary/files/document/142-1404405754-donkey_
health_and_welfare_8.pdf. Accessed March 24, 2015.

Taylor, Tex S., and Nora S. Matthews. "Donkey and Mule
Scenarios: When to Stop, Think, Read, or Call." IVIS. 2002.
www.ivis.org/proceedings/aaep/2002/910102000115.PDF.
Accessed March 29, 2015.

Watson, Tim, Han van der Kolk, Johnathon Naylor, and Gayle
Hallowell. "Hyperlipemia Syndrome." *Vet Stream.* www
.vetstream.com/equis/Content/Disease/dis00329. Accessed
June 14, 2015.

Webber, Lola, and Suzanne Rogers. "The Dependence of Humans on Working Equines (Horses, Donkeys and Mules)." *Animal Mosaic*. June 3, 2014. www.slideshare.net/EddyMwachenje/masters-research-proposal-biogs-final. Accessed April 20, 2015.

PERSONAL INTERVIEWS

Cohen, Lisa, e-mail message to author, 2015.

Davis, Jeanine, e-mail message to author, 2015.

Dawson-Graham, Heidi, e-mail message to author, 2015.

Forrester, Giselle Louise, e-mail message to author, 2015.

Freeman, Ginny, e-mail message to author, 2015

Hoffman, Shannon, e-mail message to author, 2015.

Karneffel, Rachel, e-mail message to author, 2015.

Kerson, Nancy Warrick, e-mail message to author, 2015.

Kidwell, Deb Collins, e-mail message to author, 2015.

McLean, Amy, PhD, e-mail message to author, 2015.

Morris, Linda, e-mail message to author, 2015.

Ness, Sally Anne L., DVM, DACVIM, e-mail message to author, 2015.

Osorio, Luzma, e-mail message to author, 2015.

Radcliff, Bob, personal interview with author, 2014.

Selby, Colleen, e-mail message to author, 2015.

Sullivan, Kim, e-mail message to author, 2015.

INDEX

ABOUT THE AUTHOR

Donna Campbell Smith has worked in the horse industry for more than thirty years as an instructor, trainer, breeder, and writer. She has an AAS degree in Equine Technology from Martin Community College and is a certified riding instructor. Donna also served many years as a master volunteer in the North Carolina 4-H Horse Program. She is now retired from "active" horse duties and writes from her home in North Carolina. In addition, she works as assistant to the program coordinator for the Franklin County Arts Council and was named 2011 FCAC Artist of the Year for her work in literary arts and photography.

Smith has written three non-fiction books prior to *The Book of Donkeys*: *The Book of Miniature Horses* (Lyons Press, 2005), *The Book of Draft Horses: The Horse That Built the World* (Lyons Press, 2007), and *The Book of Mules: Selecting, Breeding, and Caring for Equine Hybrids* (Lyons Press, 2009).

Smith is a freelance writer and photographer with articles and photographs published in several regional and national magazines including *The Horse, The Brayer, Western Mule, Back Home, Grit Gazette, Stable Management, USA Equestrian, Young Rider, The Chronicle of the Horse, Carolina Hoofprints, Boys' Life, The Gaited Horse, Our State, Carolina Country,* and *Conquistador.*